AF695493

TAX EXPENDITURE ESTIMATION TOOL KIT

DECEMBER 2023

ASIAN DEVELOPMENT BANK

ADB

Creative Commons Attribution 3.0 IGO license (CC BY 3.0 IGO)

© 2023 Asian Development Bank
6 ADB Avenue, Mandaluyong City, 1550 Metro Manila, Philippines
Tel +63 2 8632 4444; Fax +63 2 8636 2444
www.adb.org

Some rights reserved. Published in 2023.

ISBN 978-92-9270-551-0 (print), 978-92-9270-552-7 (electronic), 978-92-9270-553-4 (ebook)
Publication Stock No. TIM230601
DOI: http://dx.doi.org/10.22617/TIM230601

The views expressed in this publication are those of the authors and do not necessarily reflect the views and policies of the Asian Development Bank (ADB) or its Board of Governors or the governments they represent.

ADB does not guarantee the accuracy of the data included in this publication and accepts no responsibility for any consequence of their use. The mention of specific companies or products of manufacturers does not imply that they are endorsed or recommended by ADB in preference to others of a similar nature that are not mentioned.

By making any designation of or reference to a particular territory or geographic area, or by using the term "country" in this document, ADB does not intend to make any judgments as to the legal or other status of any territory or area.

This publication is available under the Creative Commons Attribution 3.0 IGO license (CC BY 3.0 IGO) https://creativecommons.org/licenses/by/3.0/igo/. By using the content of this publication, you agree to be bound by the terms of this license. For attribution, translations, adaptations, and permissions, please read the provisions and terms of use at https://www.adb.org/terms-use#openaccess.

This CC license does not apply to non-ADB copyright materials in this publication. If the material is attributed to another source, please contact the copyright owner or publisher of that source for permission to reproduce it. ADB cannot be held liable for any claims that arise as a result of your use of the material.

Please contact pubsmarketing@adb.org if you have questions or comments with respect to content, or if you wish to obtain copyright permission for your intended use that does not fall within these terms, or for permission to use the ADB logo.

Corrigenda to ADB publications may be found at http://www.adb.org/publications/corrigenda.

Note:
In this publication, "$" refers to United States dollars.

Cover design by Cleone Baradas.

CONTENTS

TABLES AND FIGURES

TABLES

FIGURES

ACKNOWLEDGMENTS

This report was led and reviewed by Sandeep Bhattacharya, senior public management specialist (tax), Asian Development Bank (ADB), and written by Selcuk Caner, tax research expert, former International Monetary Fund senior economist and ADB consultant. We wish to thank Bruno Carrasco, director general, Climate Change and Sustainable Development Department, ADB; and Hiranya Mukhopadhyay, director, Public Sector Management and Governance Sector Office (Central and West Asia and Knowledge Solutions) Sectors Group, ADB, for providing strategic guidance and comments in the development of this document. We are grateful to Janet Stotsky, tax policy expert and former International Monetary Fund staff as well as ADB consultant, for peer reviewing the document and providing invaluable comments. We thank Yolanda Lommen, advisor, Climate Change and Sustainable Development Department, ADB, for her detailed review of the draft and valuable editorial suggestions.

ABBREVIATIONS

ACE	allowance for corporate equity
ASYCUDA	Automated System for Customs Data
CCA	Capital Cost Allowance
CIT	corporate income tax
COGS	Cost of Goods Sold.
GDP	gross domestic product
ITC	Investment Tax Credit
METR	marginal effective tax rate
MPPD	Manufacturing and Processing Deduction
OECD	Organisation for Economic Co-operation and Development
PIT	personal income tax
R&D	research and development
SBD	Small Business Deduction
SEZ	special economic zone
SIC	Standard Industrial Classification
VAT	value-added tax

EXECUTIVE SUMMARY

This study reviews commonly used estimation methodologies to estimate revenues forgone resulting from tax expenditures. While the estimation methodologies are not complicated, the reliability of the estimates depends on the availability and quality of tax data. Tax expenditures are often introduced into the tax system gradually and result in significant revenue losses without much benefit to society. A comprehensive review of tax expenditures would be useful in providing guidance on the usefulness of these measures.

Widespread exemptions and preferential tax treatments, designed to protect specific categories and encourage investment in certain sectors, narrow the tax base and distort the allocation of resources. This undermines the overall equity and efficiency of the tax system and may become an obstacle for inclusive growth. Identifying and managing tax expenditures secures the integrity of a tax system by simplifying tax filing, increasing the stability of the tax system and increasing its perceived equity and efficiency.

Proper methods are required to estimate the revenue impact of tax expenditures. Revenues forgone are estimated using aggregate models, microsimulation models, distributional models, and effective tax rate methodologies. Equally important is access to the data sources that will identify and quantify the revenue losses from tax expenditures.

This tool kit serves as a guideline on the use of methodologies and models in the assessment of tax expenditures that are used by ministries of finance and tax administrations in many countries at varying degrees. The stylized models presented demonstrate how to calculate the revenues forgone under major taxes when a tax concession is introduced. Data sources and the use of the data in the models are also demonstrated. The tool kit is intended to support tax analysts in their efforts to estimate revenue losses of tax expenditures.

1 TAX EXPENDITURES

Tax systems are designed to collect revenues to finance public expenditures in the most efficient manner. Since taxes constitute a price on economic activity, the tax structure should aim to collect taxes fairly and efficiently. The tax system should be designed with an aim to minimize excess burden to the economy for the sake of efficiency. However, an efficient tax system may ignore the distribution of the tax burden among the taxpayers. Therefore, emphasis should be given to the ability to pay taxes. An equitable tax system would tax according to the ability of the taxpayers to pay their taxes. In addition, the tax system should be simple, and tax should be collected with lower compliance costs. These characteristics outline the three main principles of a tax system: efficiency, equity, and simplicity.

In addition to raising revenues for financing public expenditures, the tax system is used by governments to pursue social and economic objectives. For example, instead of making direct payments to low-income households, the government may decide to exempt their income from personal taxes or provide a tax credit. Similarly, the government may exempt a portion of income that is allocated to savings accounts, to increase the overall savings rate or stimulate investments that may not occur otherwise. In such cases, the tax system forgoes part of the tax revenues that would have been collected. This set of policy measures is referred to as tax expenditures. They are expenditures undertaken instead of direct expenditures to achieve social and economic policies.

According to the Organisation for Economic Co-operation and Development (OECD) (2004), tax expenditures are transfers of public resources carried out by reducing the tax liabilities of taxpayers relative to a tax system without the benefits to the taxpayers (the benchmark). To establish a benchmark and estimate the revenues forgone resulting from tax expenditures, tax expenditures must be identified and agreed upon. Once the benchmark is identified then, the provisions of tax legislation can be contrasted against this benchmark.

Because of the lack of an overall agreement on what constitutes universally accepted tax expenditures, estimates of tax expenditures may vary from one country to another. However, the tools used for estimating revenues forgone are based on generally accepted methodologies.

Some countries have gained experience in the design and costing of tax expenditures, and integrating tax expenditures in their annual budgets. Others provide periodic estimates of tax expenditures, while some do not estimate tax expenditures. International financial organizations encourage member countries to develop their own tax expenditure reporting practice.

Although many tax expenditure studies by different countries exist, it is not possible to compare the magnitude of the revenues forgone internationally. This is primarily due to the lack of consensus on the definition of an internationally agreed benchmark. Countries differ on what constitutes a tax expenditure and what does not. A tax expenditure item can be considered as part of the benchmark in one country while it may also be considered a divergence from the basic benchmark system. For example, a standard deduction for personal income tax may be considered part of the benchmark system while another country may see it as a tax benefit. Furthermore, data on tax expenditures may be available in one country while another country may not collect that data.

Against this background, this study does not provide an international comparison of forgone revenues, but rather presents selected tax expenditure reports and methodologies to provide a summary of how different countries approach the estimation of tax expenditures.

Tax expenditures, like budget expenditures, should have well-defined objectives such as increase capital outlays in a sector and support disposable income of low-income households, among others.[1] Without defined objectives, it is not possible to assess the effectiveness of tax expenditures as a policy tool. It is common practice to define objectives broadly, allowing for discretionary use of tax expenditures with the aim of achieving a behavioral outcome. Well-defined objectives also prevent redundancy and waste. The analysis of tax expenditures should be used to increase the efficiency of government spending programs by encouraging the repeal of wasteful programs, ensuring that government objectives are pursued with effective policy instruments.

In principle, several issues must be addressed to provide a rational justification for the existence of tax expenditures. It is key to determine whether the tax expenditure is serving a valid government objective and whether the objective reflects a government priority. In this regard, the following questions will be vital to design efficient tax expenditures: Are the benefits distributed fairly? Are the benefits well targeted to the intended beneficiaries? Does the tax expenditure cause any unintended distorting effects? Are the administrative and compliance costs of the program reasonable? How much control does the government have over the spending program? Is the program appropriately implemented? Could the objective be served better by some other policy instrument? And if the expenditure program is to be delivered through the tax system, what are the appropriate instruments to use?

While the idea of tax expenditures appears straightforward, there are difficulties in defining the benchmark against which they should be measured. In the case of income tax, the benchmark should be the broad Haig–Simons definition of comprehensive income. This benchmark would include all changes in net economic wealth in a period plus consumption in that period.[2] However, according to OECD (1996), many countries choose a benchmark that is closer to their actual tax system instead of a notional system called the "legal" approach.

Defining a benchmark raises two problems: first, reaching an agreement within the country about what constitutes a tax expenditure; and second, the lack of international comparability in tax expenditure reports. It should be noted that in the absence of international consensus on the benchmark tax system, tax provisions that are regarded as tax expenditures in some countries may not be so regarded in others.

1 For example, in the Philippines, 60% of the tax expenditures are used to support investments (GTED Database 2021). On the other hand, many developed countries such as the United Kingdom and the United States use income tax credit to support families with children in low-income groups.

2 The Haig–Simons definition of income refers to the sum of changes in the net worth and consumption. Here, the change in wealth is the savings of the taxpayer.

2 DEFINITION OF TAX EXPENDITURES AND BENCHMARKING

Definition of Tax Expenditures

The OECD defines tax expenditures as reductions in tax liabilities in comparison with a benchmark tax system and explains that they may take different forms:[3]

- Exemptions: Revenue or transactions that are excluded from the tax base. In legal regulations, these are encountered under various headings (e.g., exemptions, tax holidays, nontaxable events, etc.).
- Allowances: Amounts that can be deducted from the tax base.
- Credits: Amounts that can be deducted from the tax liability.
- Rate relief: Lower tax rates than those generally applied.
- Deferral: Postponement or delay in the tax payment.

Tax expenditures can be classified across taxes as shown in Table 1.

Table 1: Tax Expenditures by Type of Tax

Tax Expenditure Items	Taxes				
	Personal Income Tax	Corporate Profits Tax	Consumption Taxes (VAT/GST)	Excises[a]	Customs
Preferential tax rates	√	√	√		
Tax holidays		√			
Special zones		√	√		√
Capital recovery incentives		√			
Tax credits	√	√			
Treatment of dividends	√	√			
Deductions/allowances	√	√			
Exemptions	√	√	√		√
Investment subsidies		√		√	
Tax deferrals		√	√		√
Fiscal regime benefits for extractive industries		√	√	√	√

GST = goods and services tax, VAT = value-added tax.

[a] Applicable to fuels.

Source: Author.

[3] See OECD (2004) on the classification of tax expenditure groupings.

Benchmarking

The benchmark tax can be determined either based on a comprehensive methodology, the so-called *conceptual approach,* or on the so-called *legal approach*. The *conceptual approach* attempts to link the benchmark tax to a "normative tax structure," which does not necessarily bear any relation to the legal definitions of the tax (OECD 2004).

The *conceptual approach* links the benchmark tax to a "normative tax structure" that may differ from the legal definition of a tax system, and the income tax base is as defined by the Haig–Simons income concept. In the case of consumption-based taxes, the tax base becomes the total final consumption (OECD 2004).

The *legal approach* takes the current tax legislation as a basis for defining the benchmark tax and, thereby, for identifying tax expenditures. The problem with the *legal approach,* in relation to the *conceptual approach,* is that many tax concessions may not be considered tax expenditures according to how they are defined in the tax legislation. The benchmark should differ from the actual tax system to identify the tax expenditures. According to Heady and Mansour (2019), all benefits other than the basic allowance should be excluded from the benchmark. Under the corporate profits tax, the benchmark should consist of all revenues and business expenses used in arriving at profits subject to a single tax rate.[4] In addition, some tax expenditures may be introduced through different legislation, such as laws on economic zones, investments, labor, or fiscal regimes included in the contracts in extractive industries.[5] The benchmark for value-added tax (VAT) should have the broadest possible consumption base with only a zero rate on exports and a single tax rate on other goods and services. In the case of multiple tax rates, the highest rate is generally considered the benchmark rate. If capital goods and intermediate inputs are exempted, then they should be considered part of the benchmark.

In addition, there is the analogous subsidy approach that identifies as tax expenditures only those tax concessions that are equivalent to a direct subsidy (Craig and Allan 2001). In this approach, tax benefits that are of subsidy nature are considered tax expenditures. So, they would be identified like the legal approach reducing the scope of tax expenditures. The conceptual approach constitutes a wider definition than that of the other two approaches, resulting in a more extensive list of tax expenditures with a greater total cost.[6]

---

4 The issue of economic or tax depreciation may arise; however, the depreciation rates in the tax laws should not significantly differ than the economic depreciation rates.

5 High tax rates usually used in the taxation of extractive industries should not be taken as a benchmark because these high tax rates are reserved in capturing economic rents.

6 According to Craig and Allan (2001), six OECD countries apply the conceptual approach (Australia, Belgium, Canada, Finland, Ireland, and Spain); five use the legal approach (Austria, France, the Netherlands, Portugal, and the Republic of Korea); and two use the analogous subsidy approach (Germany and the United Kingdom).

3 EFFECTIVENESS AND EFFICIENCY OF TAX EXPENDITURES

Tax expenditures must be evaluated according to how the measures achieve their intended objectives. How the objectives are achieved depends on

> "(a) the characteristics of the target population (for example, characteristics of actual recipients compared with intended recipients); (b) changes in economic behavior or conditions (for example, the extent to which the tax expenditure is directly responsible for these changes, or whether other factors are responsible); and (c) the cost of the tax expenditure (for example, the amount of tax relief being provided and its actual cost relative to its expected cost" (OECD 2004).

Unintended effects should also be taken into consideration in evaluating the effectiveness of tax expenditures. To capture all intended and unintended effects of tax expenditures, various methodologies may have to be used. These may include economic impact studies and case studies and surveys, and interviews with the beneficiaries of tax benefits may be necessary.

When analyzed as government spending programs, tax expenditures often turn out not to be serving the government's intended objectives at an acceptable revenue cost, or not reflecting the government's spending priorities. In this case, it is recommended that they are repealed or restructured into a direct expenditure. For those tax expenditures serving a well-justified government objective, often some other government policy instrument, such as some form of direct spending, loan, or loan guarantee program, can more effectively achieve the objective that the tax expenditure was claimed to serve. For those tax expenditures that remain in the tax system, their design should be evaluated to ensure that they are achieving their objectives in an equitable and efficient manner. It is often possible to identify better means of indirect subsidy, such as a tax credit in the case of income taxation.

It is often argued that tax expenditures may make the tax system less fair, efficient, and simple. They make the tax system less fair by enabling some taxpayers to pay less than others with the same income or capacity to pay. They may also reduce the tax burden as a proportion of income for those with a higher ability to pay by encouraging the taxpayers to substitute activities that are tax-preferred for those that are otherwise more productive. As a result of the increased number of tax expenditures, the tax system becomes more complicated, and taxpayers may engage in rent-seeking activities as they have to navigate through detailed rules to qualify for benefits.

Tax expenditures can increase inequality. First, for example, any deduction or exemption from the income tax base has a greater monetary value to people with higher incomes because of the higher marginal tax rate that they face, and therefore the greater extent to which their tax payments are reduced. In recent years, many countries have been moving, to varying degrees, away from tax deductions toward tax credits, for which the amount of tax relief is independent of the taxpayer's marginal tax rate. Second, tax expenditures can increase inequality in that the size of a deduction for items, such as mortgage interest and pension contributions, will be greater for higher-income households, simply because these households can afford to spend more or make higher contributions for which the deductions are based.

Furthermore, tax expenditures undermine the structure built on a broad base and uniform moderate tax rate, which is regarded as less distortionary. A broad base is also easier to administer—and to comply with—since it avoids the need to distinguish between items that are taxed at the main rate and those that are taxed at a reduced (or zero) rate, or otherwise receive a tax preference, and so reduces the potential for tax avoidance. Consequently, for any given level of revenue, a broader base permits a lower rate of tax, which reduces the incentive for tax avoidance and evasion, as well as lobbying for exemptions by special-interest groups.

Broad-based uniform tax systems are advocated in principle, but in the case of negative externalities, they may not produce the least distortionary outcome because the externality can be reduced through taxation. In this case, multiple tax rates may be necessary. Selective excise duties or subsidies can supplement a VAT with a single or few rates, to discourage the activities producing a negative externality. Externalities can also be dealt with through income and other forms of tax. A reduced tax rate on savings is often justified, either through a deduction or exclusion, or lower rate of taxation, with the aim of supporting capital accumulation, which is thought to have positive externalities.[7]

A commonly accepted tax expenditure is the deductibility of the interest expense on debt. This is considered an incentive to support financing of investments by debt. The interest expense deduction has been criticized on the grounds that it distorts the financing of investments by reducing the after-tax cost of debt finance. This bias for debt finance is overcome by introducing another tax expenditure, an allowance for corporate equity (ACE). In several countries, ACE is introduced as a tax expenditure in order to make the investment finance neutral between debt and equity finance.[8] However, while this may level the field in financing, allowing for ACE deduction introduces the risk of eroding the corporate tax base,[9] which is not directly measurable. If maintaining equity between debt and equity finance is the objective, it would be more efficient and administratively simple to repeal the deductibility of interest expense.

These examples show that tax expenditures may be justified if the motivations and intentions are clear. In broad terms, tax expenditures may be classified as those that intend to modify behavior and those that redistribute income (making them equivalent to social benefit expenditures). Tax expenditures can serve as powerful instruments whether they are designed to provide incentives to modify behavior or rather to redistribute income (and so serve the same purpose as social benefits). A finer classification of tax expenditures can be as follows:

- technical tax expenditures,
- tax expenditures that redistribute income or have the same purpose as social benefits, and
- tax expenditures that are designed to modify behavior (including in-work tax credits).

Technical Tax Expenditures

Technical tax expenditures are deviations from the benchmark tax system that are justified by the need for efficiency and simplicity of tax administration. Examples include the taxation of capital gains at realization rather than accrual, and the exemption of intermediation and some financial services from VAT. These

[7] See OECD (2010).

[8] See Klemm (2006) for a description of ACE on efforts to establish tax neutrality between debt finance and equity finance.

[9] For example, Belgium and Estonia experienced significant revenue losses after allowing ACE deductions from income before taxes.

types of tax expenditures are justified because they substantially reduce administrative and compliance costs— but an attempt can be made to estimate the revenue costs.[10]

Tax Expenditures That Have the Same Purpose as Social Benefits

Many countries have tax provisions that have the same purpose as social benefits, such as tax deductions or tax credits for dependent children. The removal of these tax expenditures would typically require their replacement by ordinary expenditure programs; consequently, it would neither increase revenue nor provide an opportunity for tax rate reduction. These types of tax expenditures are justified, because (i) these tax provisions reflect ability to pay, and (ii) they may be administratively more efficient. However, they may also be designed as tax expenditures to hide their true cost to taxpayers.

Tax Expenditures That Are Designed to Modify Behavior

Tax expenditures that are designed to modify behavior are closest to the idea of a "tax incentive." Examples of such tax expenditures are tax credits for research and development (R&D), accelerated depreciation for investment, and tax deductions for interest on mortgages (unless the imputed rent from the home is subject to tax). Tax reductions that are intended to encourage increased savings would also fall into this category. To justify these types of tax expenditures, there must be a sound economic reason for change in behavior. Market failures occur because of firms and households making decisions that lead to inefficiency. Market failures are often observed in all economies, but their mere existence is not sufficient to justify intervention. It is necessary to show that the benefits of intervention (the change in behavior) outweigh the costs (administrative and compliance costs; the likely costs of unintended consequences of the intervention, including tax-planning opportunities; and the costs of diverting public funds to provide the financial incentive).

For example, R&D subsidies (whether through tax expenditures or ordinary budget expenditures) require quantification of not only the benefits of the resulting increase in R&D but also the costs of providing the funds (which may include the distortionary costs of raising additional tax revenue), the costs of administering the subsidy, and the costs of tax-planning opportunities that might arise. In addition to assessing the efficiency aspects of providing an incentive, the distributional effects should be well understood. A common criticism of financial incentives, for instance, for house purchases and pensions, is that high-income groups benefit from them and do not need the incentive. This suggests that the incentives may not improve tax effectiveness and income distribution.

Overall, some incentives can be shown to work better when delivered through the tax system than through an expenditure program. The only circumstances in which tax incentives have any claim to be more efficient are when

- the association of the incentive with the desired behavior is strengthened (as in making work pay) or correcting an externality; or
- the incentive is simply a modification of an existing tax provision (such as increasing the depreciation allowance); or
- the incentive allows administrative and compliance costs to be reduced.

---

10 While revenue losses estimates are based on realized revenues and expenditures, potential revenues can be estimated on unrealized gains. For example, capital gains accrue to real and financial assets. Potential revenues can be estimated using market value of the unrealized portion of the assets.

4 ESTIMATION METHODOLOGIES

Measurement of cost-effectiveness of tax expenditures is a key step in evaluating economic efficiency because it provides a perspective on the ability of the tax expenditure measure to improve overall real income. Cost-effectiveness is determined as the value of the change in economic benefits (welfare gain) that is directly attributable to the tax measure (i.e., its incrementality) per dollar of tax revenue forgone.[11] A tax expenditure measure is cost-effective if the tax expenditure produces sufficient aggregate activity to generate more income than the revenues forgone. In other words, the ratio of additional income generated must be greater than the revenues forgone. This implies an increase in economic efficiency because the targeted activity generates more value than the tax revenue losses.

However, the gains accruing from the introduction of tax expenditures are not limited to the immediate recipients of the benefits. There may be spillover effects elsewhere in the economy. To capture all gains, the analysis of tax expenditures should be extended to measure gains in real incomes, benefits of market correction if there is any, and additional cost incurred elsewhere in terms of higher taxes to finance the benefits and related compliance costs. Cost-effectiveness alone does not include all general equilibrium effects that may occur elsewhere in the economy. Cost-effectiveness estimates may not be sufficient indicators of efficiency because they do not capture all the benefits and costs of tax expenditures. Nevertheless, partial-equilibrium estimates provide a good indicator of the economic benefits to the targeted taxpayer groups.

It is good practice to provide estimates of economic benefits of tax expenditures, but the methodology employed in this tool kit focuses on the description of methods used in estimating the revenues forgone. The revenues forgone are commonly estimated using one of the three approaches: *revenue forgone*, *revenue gain*, and *outlay equivalent*. These estimates can be calculated either on a cash-flow or accrual basis. The measurements are the main components of a tax expenditure report.

The ***revenue forgone*** method is an ex post calculation of the loss in revenue incurred by the government. It does not consider taxpayers' behavioral responses.[12] For example, if the tax benefit is a tax credit, the revenue forgone would be the amount of the tax credit received by the taxpayer. Similarly, the revenue loss because of a tax deduction is the amount of the deduction allowed as a tax expenditure times the marginal tax rate. Most developing countries estimate tax expenditures using the revenue foregone approach for which data are more readily available.

[11] See Beer et al. (2022) and Phillips, Tyskerud, and Warwick (2021) on the estimation of economic costs and benefits of tax expenditures.

[12] For definition of revenues forgone, see OECD (2004).

The ***revenue gain*** method is an ex ante calculation of the additional revenue that would accrue from repealing tax expenditures with taxpayers' behavioral responses (OECD 2004). This method requires modeling the taxpayer behavior using price elasticities of supply and demand. Compared to the revenue forgone method, the revenue gains method estimates revenues gained by eliminating the tax expenditures after the behavioral responses are accounted for. The application of this method is limited because of the need to estimate the price elasticities of supply and demand of the beneficiaries of tax expenditures.

For example, in the case of VAT, the VAT rate—normally around 15%–18%—may be reduced to a lower rate on new housing construction. When the benefit is repealed, the revenue gained may not equal the revenue forgone. Due to a price response, purchases may decline, and the resulting revenue gains may be less than the expected value. In this case, accurate price elasticities of demand and supply have to be estimated to account for the price response, which may not be possible. Therefore, this approach is not generally used in tax expenditure studies.

The third approach is the ***outlay equivalent*** (equivalent direct expenditure) method. It calculates the outlay that would have resulted in a similar gain for the taxpayer as the considered tax expenditure (OECD 2004). Assume, for example, that corporate profits before taxes and R&D expenditures are 100 each. The tax code allows for an additional deduction of 50% of R&D expenditures. Allowing for an additional deduction of 50 (50% of 100) from taxable corporate income reduces the corporate tax liability from 40 to 20. Under the revenue forgone method, the cost of allowing for an additional 50% of R&D expenses would be 20. Under the equivalent outlay method, revenue forgone would be 20 if the tax benefit is not subject to corporate income tax. But the equivalent amount would be 33.33 (20/(1 – 0.4) = 33.33) if the tax benefit is subject to corporate income tax.[13]

Tax deferrals are also considered tax expenditures because current tax liabilities are postponed into an uncertain future. Depreciation allowances that differ from accepted accounting principles or tax accounting rules are postponement of tax liabilities. Revenues forgone are estimated by taking the present value of the tax benefit over the depreciation period of the asset.

[13] Outlay equivalent = revenue forgone/(1 – tax rate).

5 MEASUREMENT METHODOLOGIES OF TAX EXPENDITURES AND DATA SOURCES

All methods and models measure the revenue forgone resulting from a tax expenditure item that is a benefit to the taxpayer. These methods and models vary from using a simulation model based on aggregated taxpayer data, indirect methods using data from sources external to the tax administration such as the national accounts or surveys, and microsimulation models using individual taxpayer data.[14] The estimations are done generally by removing a tax expenditure item from the calculations of tax liability.

Simulations based on aggregate tax data include calculation of the tax liability on aggregated taxpayer data excluding the tax expenditure benefits. Indirect estimation of revenue forgone uses data obtained from national accounts or household surveys, and creates and calculates the tax liability with and without the tax expenditures. This is used whenever a change would affect a section of the economy that does not currently file returns (for example, if an income tax exemption is in place for farmers and they are not required to report their agricultural income). Calculating the expenditure incurred on exempting this form of income cannot be done using taxpayer data or returns as they are not current taxpayers or filers. Microsimulation models use individual taxpayer data either from a sample or the full taxpayer population. In addition to estimating the revenue forgone, microsimulation models provide information on the distributional impact of tax expenditures. Out of the three methods of estimation of tax expenditures, microsimulation models are the most powerful estimation tools.

Calculation Methods for Estimating Revenues Forgone

Revenue effects of tax expenditures can be estimated using various methods ranging from individually recorded tax benefits to methods applied to aggregate national data. The estimates depend on the types of tax expenditures and the availability of data.[15]

Direct Data Collection from Revenue Statistics

Some tax expenditures may be recorded separately for each beneficiary by tax administrations. Tax credits, investment allowances, or additional depreciation allowances may be recorded either on a tax return or registered separately in a registry. In this case, the revenues forgone can be directly compiled from these entries. This requires additional effort in designing tax forms or developing databases when implemented by tax administrations.

Estimates Using Aggregate Statistics

Estimates are based on aggregate tax statistics, obtained from summary tax return statistics and sources such as national accounts, household surveys, and business surveys. If the revenues forgone can be calculated by multiplying the total value of tax expenditures expressed as a proportion of aggregate statistics, the resulting estimate would be fairly accurate.

[14] The data can be the population of all taxpayers or a sample of taxpayers representing all the taxpayers.

[15] For further description of calculation methods, see Brown (2004).

For example, revenues forgone because of exemptions and deductions from corporate income taxation can be estimated by multiplying the aggregate amount of deductions or exemptions by the statutory corporate income tax rate. Similarly, revenues forgone resulting from exemptions and deductions on personal income tax can also be estimated using the same method. The aggregate amount of the deduction or exempted incomes can be multiplied by a marginal weighted average tax rate (due to a progressive rate structure). The marginal weighted average tax rate must be calculated separately. It may be necessary to calculate a different marginal weighted average tax rate for each deduction or exemption because the beneficiaries of each type of tax exemption, such as medical deductions, may be subject to different marginal tax rates.[16] Use of aggregated data provides a reasonable estimate of the revenues forgone even though it may not be as precise as simulation models.

Aggregate Simulation Models

Both aggregate tax data and data from national accounts can be incorporated into an aggregate simulation model. For example, input–output tables, compiled by national statistics agencies, will provide a comprehensive economic database for analyzing the effects of changes in a particular industry on others. A tax benefit for a particular industry will reduce its cost structure and increase its sales to and purchases from other industries. Therefore, aggregated corporate tax deductions or exemptions can be incorporated into the input–output tables to estimate their economic benefits.

Input–output models provide precise estimation of revenues forgone because of tax exemptions under the VAT system.[17] In fact, input–output models would be more appropriate than microsimulation models based on tax returns in mimicking the VAT's payment system where VAT charged is offset by VAT paid on inputs. In addition, revenues forgone, as a result of an exemption, depend not only on the taxpayer exempted but also on whether the buyer from the taxpayer is a final consumer or an exempt intermediate purchaser. For estimating revenues forgone resulting from VAT exemptions, zero-rating or preferential tax rate input–output models would be more appropriate. These models can enable the incorporation of all the features of the VAT system. The revenues forgone are estimated by taking the difference between the VAT liability under a benchmark and the VAT liability without the VAT expenditures.

Microsimulation Models

Microsimulation models are used to calculate tax liability by repeating the same tax calculations on each taxpayer's tax data. The calculated tax liability for each taxpayer is summed up to obtain the total tax liability. It is also possible to append additional data to each observation in the data file from external sources such as household expenditure surveys for individuals or financial statements for corporations. Some countries include all the tax data in microsimulations, while others use a sample of taxpayer data that is representative of the total population of taxpayers. While using the full population of taxpayers is computationally feasible, the accuracy gains are not much. Instead, using a representative sample of taxpayers would be quicker to estimate the cost of tax expenditures. Furthermore, with close editing of the sampled tax returns, the taxpayer data would be more likely to be error free.

16 For example, the marginal weighted average tax rate applicable for medical deductions may differ from the marginal weighted average tax rate for mortgage interest expense deductions due to the income characteristics of the recipients of both benefits.

17 For example, Australia uses an input–output model to estimate the revenue effects of tax concessions (Brown 2004).

Microsimulation models calculate the tax liability for all the taxpayers included in the data file under the current tax law. Then, the same liability is calculated without the tax expenditures individually. Revenue forgone is calculated as the difference between the tax liability under the current law and the calculated tax liability excluding the tax expenditures form the tax liability calculations. In addition to estimating the revenue cost of tax expenditures, microsimulation models enable the distribution of revenue effects of tax expenditures by income group, industry group, type of income, and region.

The data for microsimulation models are obtained from tax returns from a particular year, most often, the most recent year with complete data. Updating and adjusting the microsimulation databases is labor-intensive and time-consuming. Thus, updating procedures are needed to adjust the database to reflect the taxpayer population in future years. Updating procedures may vary from applying simple growth rates to data to more sophisticated procedures targeting an aggregate tax liability level while minimizing the variations in the data.

Microsimulation models are useful tools for detailed analysis of the characteristics of the taxpayer population. Some of these features are not easily observable in aggregate statistics, therefore, they result in the better understanding of the outcomes of tax expenditure measures. Microsimulation models are also useful in estimating parameters such as tax elasticities by type of households or industries that can be used in aggregate models. For example, marginal effective tax rates can be easily calculated using a microsimulation model. Then, the marginal effective tax rate can be applied in aggregate estimation of the revenue effects of tax expenditures. Commonly used microsimulation models for assessing tax expenditures are

- personal income tax microsimulation model,
- corporate income tax microsimulation model, and
- aggregate simulation model for indirect taxes (VAT and excises).

A typical microsimulation model comprises three elements: (1) a micro-level database (typically information from tax returns for individuals or corporations for the base year and future years for income tax calculations and sales and purchase data for consumption taxes), and its assumptions about the system; (2) a tax calculator (an algorithm that calculates the tax liability under alternative tax structures and which may be supplemented with behavioral changes associated with the tax changes); and (3) an output program that categorizes taxes paid by income group, tax burdens, winners and losers, and the overall change in revenue (Brown 2004).

The core of the model is the micro data, which serve as the observation units of the model. The data can be tax data of firms in the case of corporate income tax or individuals for personal income tax.

Micro-level database. The data for microsimulation models should come from a fully representative sample of taxpayers—individuals or corporations—and contain all available information from the tax returns or other reporting documents such as annual sales tax reconciliation reports or property tax records.
The sampling procedures used for database development should be sophisticated enough to ensure an accurate reflection of the true population. If the population (whether firms or individuals) is relatively homogeneous, a basic random sample of the population is probably sufficient to ensure an accurate sample. If the income distribution is highly skewed, i.e., certain industries are a much larger component of the population, or the distribution of tax liability is skewed by size of firm, then stratified sampling should be

employed. The actual type of stratification is largely determined by the characteristics of the population of taxpayers.

Figure 1: Structure of a Microsimulation Model

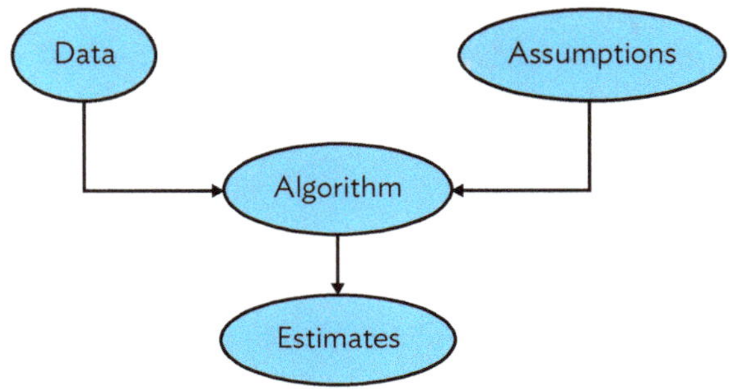

Source: Author's representation.

Tax calculator. The tax calculator is an algorithm that calculates the tax liability for each individual observation in the dataset, given the tax parameters. The algorithm reflects the calculations that taxpayers make when computing their tax liability. A tax calculator would serve to calculate the revenue under repeal of different tax expenditure items.

Output. The output of microsimulation models most typically include the following tables by income/gross revenue/SIC code group: (i) distribution of tax burdens under current law, (ii) distribution of tax burdens resulting from removal of a tax expenditure, and (iii) change in tax liability.[18] Summary output includes total revenue impacts and summary statistics by income class (including deductions, taxes paid, total income, etc.) or by industry.

Personal Income Tax

Generally Accepted Tax Expenditures Under Personal Income Tax

Following the legal approach and assuming a comprehensive personal income tax (PIT) that includes wages and salaries, capital income, business income, and pension income, the benchmark should be based on the income tax system with the statutory tax schedule.[19] The benchmark should exclude any tax relief, other than the basic allowance (or the zero-tax income bracket). Accordingly, any deduction from income (other than genuine business expenses, if the person has income from a business activity); tax credits; and lower rates on certain income (for example, capital gains, interest, dividends) are arguably tax expenditures (Heady and Mansour 2019).

Revenue losses occur as a result of a benefit in the form of a deviation from the benchmark in

- rates—including special rates on capital gains and dividends,
- inclusion or exclusion of various types of income,
- exemption amounts and a broad variety of exemption types,
- standard deduction amounts and a broad variety of standard deduction types and phase-outs,
- itemized deductions and deduction phase-outs, and
- credits such as earned-income and child-care credits.

[18] SIC stands for Standard Industrial Classification and is used for classifying industries.

[19] In some countries, mostly Northern European countries, where a dual-income tax system exists, income from labor and capital are taxed separately. In this case, it is necessary to have one benchmark for labor income and another for capital income.

Income taxes can be schedular or dual.[20] In schedular systems,[21] there would be no one PIT rate structure. Each income type would be subject to a different tax rate structure. For example, labor income, business income, and income from real estate may have their own tax rate structure. Nordic countries apply a dual tax system where wage income and capital income have different tax rate schedules. In the cases of schedular or dual income tax systems, when calculating the revenue cost of tax expenditures, separate benchmarks would be needed for each type of income. The benchmark for labor income may be similar to a benchmark for PIT, and the benchmark for capital income may be a flat tax rate.

Estimation Methodology for Tax Expenditures

A typical tax return for an individual or a household would consist of sources of income, deductions and exemptions, credits, a flat or a schedular tax rate, and calculated tax liability. The revenue impact of various tax expenditures can be analyzed with the use of an aggregate or a microsimulation model. The model would be capable of capturing revenues forgone resulting from a tax expenditure individually. Comprehensive revenue estimates can also be provided; however, in this case the interactions between tax expenditures have to be taken into account.

Table 2 displays the components of income and tax expenditure items of a hypothetical taxpayer. The tax rate schedule for income and capital gains are included at the bottom of the table. Column A represents the components of income, deductions, exemptions, and credits under the current tax provisions. The current rate structure is considered part of the benchmark. However, a preferential tax rate on capital gains would be a tax expenditure. Repealing the preferential tax rate for capital gains, all deductions, exemptions, and credits establish the benchmark. The introduction of any of these items would be a deviation from the benchmark. Columns A to H demonstrate the revenue effect of individual tax expenditure items.

The revenue effect of each tax expenditure is calculated separately. Capital gains are taxed at a lower rate of 10%. The revenue forgone from this tax expenditure is calculated by adding capital gains to taxable income and taxing at rates subject to other income. In Column B, capital gains tax is zero, but the total tax liability increased by 1,250, which is the value of the tax expenditure. The revenue impact of repealing other tax expenditures is calculated similarly, i.e., repealing the benefit and recalculating the tax liability by applying the schedular tax rates. The weighted average tax rate is the sum of the marginal tax rates applicable for each tax bracket weighted by the share of the taxable income in that bracket.[22]

20 The dual income tax is a particular form of schedular income tax in which labor income is taxed at progressive tax rates and capital income is taxed at a flat low tax rate. The flat rate on capital income is often set equal to the corporate tax rate on profits.

21 In a schedular tax system, incomes from different sources are taxed separately (i.e., under a different schedule); thus, separate tax liabilities are calculated for corporate profits, wages and salaries, income from securities and shares, rental income, etc. Alternatively, a global income tax system aggregates income from all sources at the taxpayer level. The income is then taxed at a progressive rate.

22 The weighted average tax rate is $t_w = t_1 * w_1 + t_2 * w_2 + t_3 * w_3$, where t_i is the marginal tax rate in income bracket i and w_i is the weight of the income in income bracket i. The weights are calculated by dividing the total income in income bracket i by total income. In this example, the weighted average is calculated as 15%*(30/80.9) +25%*[(75-30)/80.9]+35%*[(80.9-75)/80.9].

Table 2: Hypothetical Personal Income Tax Return and Its Components

Personal Income Tax (PIT) Components	Current Law	Repeal Preferential Capital Gains Tax Rate	Revenue Effect of Repealing Pension Contributions	Revenue Effect of Repealing Medical Expense Deduction	Revenue Effect of Repealing Mortgage Interest Deduction	Revenue Effect of Repealing Educational Expense Deduction	Revenue Effect of Repealing Exemption of Foreign Income	Revenue Effect of Repealing Earned Income Credit
	A	B	C	D	E	F	G	H
Income components	110,000	115,000	110,000	110,000	110,000	110,000	110,000	110,000
Wages and salaries	100,000	100,000	100,000	100,000	100,000	100,000	100,000	100,000
Capital gains	5,000	5,000	5,000	5,000	5,000	5,000	5,000	5,000
Interest income	1,000	1,000	1,000	1,000	1,000	1,000	1,000	1,000
Pension income	1,000	1,000	1,000	1,000	1,000	1,000	1,000	1,000
Royalties	0	0	0	0	0	0	0	0
Rental Income	3,000	3,000	3,000	3,000	3,000	3,000	3,000	3,000
Business income	5,000	5,000	5,000	5,000	5,000	5,000	5,000	5,000
Deductions	28,500	28,500	22,500	25,500	18,500	23,500	28,500	28,500
Pension contributions	6,000	6,000	0	6,000	6,000	6,000	6,000	6,000
Medical expenses	3,000	3,000	3,000	0	3,000	3,000	3,000	3,000
Mortgage interest expense	10,000	10,000	10,000	10,000	0	10,000	10,000	10,000
Educational expenses	5,000	5,000	5,000	5,000	5,000	0	5,000	5,000
Charitable donations	500	500	500	500	500	500	500	500
Business expenses	4,000	4,000	4,000	4,000	4,000	4,000	4,000	4,000
Exemptions	600	601	600	600	600	600	500	600
Exempt 50% of pension income	500	500	500	500	500	500	500	500
Foreign earned income	100	101	100	100	100	100	0	100
Taxable income	80,900	85,899	86,900	83,900	90,900	85,900	81,000	80,900
Capital gains tax @10%	500	0	500	500	500	500	500	500
Tax before credits	18,315	19,565	20,415	19,365	21,815	20,065	18,350	18,315
Credits	4,000	4,000	4,000	4,000	4,000	4,000	4,000	1,000
Child credit	1,000	1,000	1,000	1,000	1,000	1,000	1,000	1,000
Earned income credit	3,000	3,000	3,000	3,000	3,000	3,000	3,000	0
Tax after credits	14,315	15,565	16,415	15,365	17,815	16,065	14,350	17,315
Revenue forgone		1,250	2,100	1,050	3,500	1,750	35	3,000
Tax rate schedule								
0 to 30,000	15%							
30,001 to 75,000	25%							
75,000+	35%							
Weighted average tax rate	22%							
Capital gains tax rate	10%							

Source: Author's calculations.

Hypothetical Calculation of Each Type of Tax Expenditure

Aggregate Approach

The revenues forgone under each one of the tax expenditure items can be estimated by obtaining the total value of the tax expenditure and applying the weighted average tax rate to this value. Table 3 shows the aggregate tax expenditure items and the total revenue forgone in a hypothetical country. As shown in Table 3, capital gains have a preferential tax rate of 10%. The total value of capital gains income earned in a particular year can be obtained from tax returns statistics for the total population of taxpayers compiled by the tax administration. In this case, the top marginal tax rate of 35% is applied to the total value of capital gains. It is assumed that capital gains are more likely to be realized by high-income taxpayers, therefore the top marginal tax rate is applied.

In the case of deductions such as pensions contributions and medical expenses, the weighted average tax rate is used. Since these deductions are likely to be taken by all taxpayers, the appropriate tax rate would be the weighted average tax rate.

Calculated total revenues forgone, as a result of a tax benefit, are reported in column C in Table 4 as the product of the total value of the tax benefit and the statutory tax rate or the weighted average tax rate.

Microsimulation Model

Microsimulation models use micro data, and for this reason they are called microsimulation models. Microsimulation models would use the full information available on a tax return and mimic the tax calculation to determine the tax liability for each taxpayer in the data file. The data file used for simulations can be either the total population of taxpayers or a representative sample of taxpayers. If a sample is used, the estimates have to be grossed up to the population by the weights that are assigned to each taxpayer in the sample.

Microsimulation models can be developed with varying degrees of complexity, but they would all have a parameter template that would include all needed parameters to calculate the tax liability for each observation in the data file. A parameter template in a microsimulation model may look like the one in Table 4.

Table 3: Estimates of Revenue Forgone of Selected Tax Expenditure Items

	Total Value	Tax Rate	Revenue Forgone
Tax Expenditure	A	B	C = A*B
Capital gains	500,000,000	35%	175,000,000
Pension contributions	200,000,000	22%	44,042,027
Medical expense deduction	100,000,000	22%	22,021,014
Mortgage interest deduction	15,000,000	22%	3,303,152
Educational expense deduction	150,000,000	22%	33,031,520
Exempt foreign income	5,000,000	22%	1,101,051
Earned income credit	300,000,000	NA	300,000,000
Weighted average tax rate		22%	

NA = not applicable.

Source: Author's calculations.

Table 4: Parameter Template of a Personal Income Tax Microsimulation Model

Macroeconomic Variables							
		2019/20		**2020/21**		**Cumulative Factor**	
		< 65	65 >	< 65	65 >	< 65	65 >
Growth in number of taxpayers		0.0%	0.0%	0.0%	0.0%	100.0%	100.0%
Growth in income (% change in wage bill)		0.0%	0.0%	0.0%	0.0%	100.0%	100.0%
REBATE	Primary		1,700	17,000			
	65 >(Age 65 and older additional to primary rebate)		0				

TAX TABLE		**Taxable Income in LC**		**Tax Rates**	**Tax Liability**
		–	10,000	10.00%	–
		10,000	20,000	15.00%	1,000
		20,000	30,000	20.00%	2,500
		30,000	100,000	30.00%	4,500
		100,000	200,000	30.00%	25,500
	LC = Local currency	200,000		30.00%	55,500

Tax Threshold		Below age 65	Age 65 and over		
		17,000	17,000	17,000	
		Estimated total taxable income	Estimated total adjusted number of taxpayer filers		Total estimated tax
Below age 65	< 65	–	1		–
Age 65 and over	65 >	–	–		–
Total		–	**1**		–

DEDUCTION PARAMETERS		**0 OR 1**
HOUSE MAINTENANCE		1
MORTGAGE		1
DEPENDENT MEDICAL		0
OTHER DEDUCTIONS		1
PERSONAL ALLOWANCE		1
SPOUSE ALLOWANCE		1
FUTURE BENEFITS		1

Source: Author.

The tax calculator, which is the main component of the model, would take the parameters shown in Table 4 and apply them on each observation in the data file. The data file may look similar to the one shown in Table 5. In Table 5, each line contains data on the sources of income, deductions, and credits for a taxpayer. Tax liability for each line is calculated similarly as shown in Table 2. By changing the parameters in Table 5, the model would recalculate the tax liability under each scenario that repeals a tax expenditure item. In Table 5, the result of repealing medical expense deduction is simulated.

Baseline:

Taxable Income = Total income – House maintenance – Mortgage interest deduction – dependent medical deduction – Other deductions – Personal allowance – Spouse allowance – Future benefits (Social insurance premiums)

Tax Liability (Before disallowing any tax expenditure) = Taxable Income*(Tax Rate Structure)

Repealing tax expenditure: dependent medical expense deductions:

Taxable Income (disallow dependent medical expense) = Total income – House maintenance – Mortgage interest deduction – Other deductions – Personal allowance – Spouse allowance – Future benefits (Social insurance premiums)

Tax Liability (After disallowing tax expenditure) = Taxable Income*(Tax Rate Structure)

Revenue forgone = Tax Liability (After disallowing tax expenditure) – Tax Liability (Before disallowing tax expenditure)

Since the calculations are on a large dataset, the results have to be summarized and tabulated in an output file to assess the revenue forgone estimate by size of income. One important advantage of estimating revenue forgone with a microsimulation model is that it provides a distribution of the revenue impact. The outcome of the microsimulation model would show the revenue forgone of a particular tax expenditure and its distribution. Table 6 demonstrates the revenue loss of allowing a deduction for medical expenses and its distribution by size of income.

According to the results, the revenue cost of medical expense is about 8.5 million local currency (LC) or 2.2% of tax liability. The results also indicate that the primary beneficiaries of the medical expense deduction are middle- to lower-income taxpayers. The revenue cost of other tax expenditures can also be estimated similarly by changing the parameters in the parameter template.

Discussion of Data Sources

For aggregate estimates, summary data for each item reported on tax returns are available at tax administrations. If not, household expenditure surveys can be used to obtain a proxy for some tax expenditure items such as medical and education expenses. Household surveys usually report average household expenditures, so these values have to be grossed up to the population.

For microsimulation modeling purposes, the tax data may come from two different sources. One data source is the annual tax returns submitted to the revenue administrations. The other source is the survey data. Survey data are collected either by the national statistics agencies or private business services providers. Survey data would be very useful in complementing the tax return data, especially when the tax returns are not properly filed.

Table 5: Taxpayer Data as Input for the Personal Income Tax Microsimulation Model

Assessment Number	Public Sector Wages	Private Sector Wages	Business Income	Total Income	House Maintenance	Mortgage	Dependent Medical	Other Deductions	Personal Allowance	Spouse Allowance	Future Benefits	Allowances and Deductions	Taxable Income Before Personal Allowance	Total Tax Liability
792365	0	28,095	0	28,095			2,400	0	17,000	0	1,405	20,805	24,290	1,224
724151	28,098	0	0	28,098	0	0	750	0	17,000	0	1,398	19,148	25,950	1,225
763866	0	28,100	0	28,100			400	410	17,000	0	1,360	19,170	25,930	1,171
777179	28,103	0	0	28,103			400	0	17,000	1,500	1,405	20,305	24,798	1,007
765346	0	28,107	0	28,107			1,832	475	17,000	0	1,366	20,673	24,434	1,162
724158	0	28,112	0	28,112	0	0	1,100	0	17,000	0	1,400	19,500	25,612	1,227
753821	0	28,112	0	28,112			400	0	17,000	0	1,317	18,717	26,395	1,239
747028	25,177	2,936	0	28,113			1,458	0	17,000	0	2,631	21,089	24,024	1,048
752158	0	28,114	0	28,114			637	0	17,000	0	1,275	18,912	26,202	1,246
729267	0	28,115	0	28,115			4,100	0	17,000	1,500	1,395	23,995	21,120	1,010
752663	0	28,115	0	28,115	0		7,400	0	17,000	0	1,490	25,890	19,225	1,214
761607	0	28,116	0	28,116			400	2,138	17,000	0	1,814	21,352	23,764	904
773128		28,120	0	28,120			3,290		17,000	0	3,213	23,503	21,617	976
769076	0	28,125	0	28,125			3,750	0	17,000	0	1,406	22,156	22,969	1,228
759448	28,127	0	0	28,127			400	445	17,000	0	0	17,845	27,282	1,368
750801	0	28,128	0	28,128			3,400	0	17,000	0	2,030	22,430	22,698	1,138
759314	0	28,130	0	28,130			750	0	17,000	0	2,520	20,270	24,860	1,067
740735	0	24,757	3,382	28,139	0	17,229	3,750	17,343	17,000	0	4,226	42,319	17,000	0
772690	0	28,140	0	28,140			1,696	2,786	17,000	0	1,272	22,754	22,386	896
761488	0	28,141	0	28,141			3,700	1,539	17,000	0	1,891	24,130	21,011	957
751345	0	28,144	0	28,144			1,750	0	17,000	0	1,407	20,157	24,987	1,231
773556	28,144	0	0	28,144			1,100	0	17,000	0	331	18,431	26,713	1,388
741366	0	28,146	0	28,146			770	0	17,000	0	3,453	21,223	23,923	956
736587	0	28,149	0	28,149			750	0	17,000	0	1,407	19,157	25,992	1,232

Note: The data are extracted from a large dataset that contains all the taxpayers.

Source: Author.

Table 6: Output of Repealing Medical Expense Deduction

Income Category		Total Number of Taxpayers	Total Income	Taxable Income	Tax Liability	Effective Tax Rate on Total Income (%)	Effective Tax Rate on Taxable Income (%)	Share of Total Income (%)	Share of Tax Liability (%)
<	0	150	-2,455,089.9	–	–			-0.3	0.0
0	5,000	1,241	1,303,175	–	–	0.0		0.2	0.0
5,001	10,000	898	6,960,091	–	–	0.0		0.8	0.0
10,001	15,000	1,403	17,839,742	–	–	0.0		2.1	0.0
15,001	20,000	2,096	37,195,886	1,068,431	106,843	0.3	10.0	4.4	0.1
20,001	25,000	2,156	48,565,836	7,226,528	722,653	1.5	10.0	5.7	1.0
25,001	30,000	2,291	62,810,940	15,986,483	1,626,408	2.6	10.2	7.4	2.2
30,001	35,000	1,479	48,110,782	16,114,258	1,784,412	3.7	11.1	5.7	2.4
35,001	40,000	1,930	71,877,995	26,931,376	3,217,581	4.5	11.9	8.5	4.4
40,001	45,000	1,365	58,158,903	24,500,212	3,207,044	5.5	13.1	6.9	4.3
45,001	50,000	868	41,311,240	17,627,309	2,487,149	6.0	14.1	4.9	3.4
50,001	60,000	2,006	109,480,959	51,041,285	8,086,574	7.4	15.8	12.9	11.0
60,001	80,000	1,654	113,524,854	57,936,434	10,945,103	9.6	18.9	13.4	14.8
80,001	100,000	687	61,194,808	36,646,129	8,002,524	13.1	21.8	7.2	10.8
100,001	200,000	867	113,936,022	77,343,304	19,329,783	17.0	25.0	13.5	26.2
200,001	500,000	179	50,442,174	43,772,479	12,326,244	24.4	28.2	6.0	16.7
500,001	+	9	6,837,327	6,725,237	1,972,571	28.9	29.3	0.8	2.7
Total		21,279	847,095,644	382,919,465	73,814,888	8.71	19.28	100.0	100.0

Income Category		Total Number of Taxpayers	Total Income	Taxable Income	Tax Liability	Effective Tax Rate on Total Income (%)	Effective Tax Rate on Taxable Income (%)	Share of Total Income (%)	Share of Tax Liability (%)
<	0	150	-1,691,230	–	–			-0.2	0.0
0	5,000	1,241	1,303,175	–	–	0.0		0.2	0.0
5,001	10,000	898	6,960,091	–	–	0.0		0.8	0.0
10,001	15,000	1,403	17,839,742	–	–	0.0		2.1	0.0
15,001	20,000	2,096	37,195,886	2,361,678	236,168	0.6	10.0	4.4	0.3
20,001	25,000	2,156	48,565,836	10,578,002	1,057,800	2.2	10.0	5.7	1.3
25,001	30,000	2,291	62,810,940	20,170,446	2,090,330	3.3	10.4	7.4	2.5
30,001	35,000	1,479	48,110,782	19,207,274	2,213,096	4.6	11.5	5.7	2.7
35,001	40,000	1,930	71,877,995	31,388,602	3,889,420	5.4	12.4	8.5	4.7
40,001	45,000	1,365	58,158,903	27,831,901	3,785,575	6.5	13.6	6.9	4.6
45,001	50,000	868	41,311,240	19,856,282	2,915,760	7.1	14.7	4.9	3.5
50,001	60,000	2,006	109,480,959	57,129,667	9,502,531	8.7	16.6	12.9	11.5
60,001	80,000	1,654	113,524,854	63,905,369	12,463,871	11.0	19.5	13.4	15.1
80,001	100,000	687	61,194,808	39,393,866	8,782,749	14.4	22.3	7.2	10.7
100,001	200,000	867	113,936,022	81,798,343	20,645,786	18.1	25.2	13.4	25.1
200,001	500,000	179	50,442,174	44,984,595	12,689,879	25.2	28.2	5.9	15.4
500,001	+	9	6,837,327	6,888,709	2,021,613	29.6	29.3	0.8	2.5
Total		21,279	847,859,503	425,494,732	82,294,577	9.71	19.34	100.0	100.0

continued on next page

Table 6 *continued*

Income Category		Total Number of Taxpayers	Change in Total Income	Change in Taxable Income	Change in Total Tax: Total Taxpayers	Share of Change in Income (%)	Share of Change in Tax Liability (%)	% Change in Income (%)	% Change in Tax Liability (%)	Change in Effective Tax Rate on Taxable Income (%)
<	0	150	763,859.45	–	–	100.00	0			
0	5,000	1,241	–	–	–	0.00	0	0.00		
5,001	10,000	898	–	–	–	0.00	0	0.00		
10,001	15,000	1,403	–	–	–	0.00	0	0.00		
15,001	20,000	2,096	–	1,293,247	129,325	0.00	1.5	0.00	12.10	0.00
20,001	25,000	2,156	–	3,351,474	335,147	0.00	4.0	0.00	4.64	0.00
25,001	30,000	2,291	–	4,183,963	463,922	0.00	5.5	0.00	2.90	0.19
30,001	35,000	1,479	–	3,093,016	428,684	0.00	5.1	0.00	2.66	0.45
35,001	40,000	1,930	–	4,457,226	671,838	0.00	7.9	0.00	2.49	0.44
40,001	45,000	1,365	–	3,331,689	578,531	0.00	6.8	0.00	2.36	0.51
45,001	50,000	868	–	2,228,972	428,611	0.00	5.1	0.00	2.43	0.57
50,001	60,000	2,006	–	6,088,382	1,415,957	0.00	16.7	0.00	2.77	0.79
60,001	80,000	1,654	–	5,968,935	1,518,768	0.00	17.9	0.00	2.62	0.61
80,001	100,000	687	–	2,747,737	780,225	0.00	9.2	0.00	2.13	0.46
100,001	200,000	867	–	4,455,039	1,316,003	0.00	15.5	0.00	1.70	0.25
200,001	500,000	179	–	1,212,116	363,635	0.00	4.3	0.00	0.83	0.05
500,001	+	9	–	163,471	49,041	0.00	0.6	0.00	0.73	0.02
Total		21,279	763,859	42,575,267	8,479,689	100.00	1	0.09	2.21	0.06

– = no value, + = over.

Source: Author's calculations.

In a general-purpose survey conducted regularly such as the household income and expenditure survey, one obtains data on the demographic and economic characteristics of the population.[23] Such a survey provides information not only about the total population but also about the subgroups of the population including gender, educational attainment, employment conditions, and income levels. The benefits of surveys are (i) data coverage from different segments of the population; and (ii) the results are representative, accurate, and reliable. In the case of PIT, some expenditures such as educational expenses may not be captured in the tax returns. These data can be captured from household income and expenditure surveys that provide detailed data on all types of incomes and expenditures. The survey data are representative of the population by income and demographics. Average values of tax expenditure items can be estimated and used to augment the taxpayer files.

[23] General-purpose surveys are conducted regularly by national statistics agencies. Household income and expenditure surveys are held nationally and contain many questions about the well-being of households. Because these surveys are not done for tax purposes, the income and expenditure data must be calibrated to reproduce aggregate tax liabilities close to actual tax liability.

Corporate Income Tax

Generally Accepted Tax Expenditures Under Corporate Income Tax

Estimating forgone revenue under corporate income tax (CIT) laws is not generally easy because of the complexity of provisions included in the tax laws. Corporations are very responsive in their behavior to the economic environment and the provisions of the tax laws. Tax bases of corporations may change in response to economic conditions and the provisions of the tax laws. Corporate tax returns often contain dynamic and nonlinear elements. Examples of dynamic and nonlinear components are net operating loss carryovers, rules for computing and claiming tax credits (nonlinear), the minimum corporate income tax provisions (nonlinear), depreciation allowances, interest deductions, and tax credit limitations.

Even a microsimulation CIT model may be inadequate to estimate the revenue cost of tax expenditures. Tax expenditure provisions such as net operating losses and depreciation allowances are very important instruments for corporations for minimizing their tax liability.[24] Nevertheless, it is possible to make static estimates of the lost revenues using aggregate corporate data or national accounts. However, microsimulation model results may differ from the revenue loss estimates obtained by aggregate methods. Table 7 demonstrates summary income and deduction items of a hypothetical corporation. These data are provided on the tax returns of the corporations. The tax accounting data consist of components of income, cost of goods sold (or COGS); deductions; allowances; net operating losses from previous years; and various forms of credits, mostly investment tax credits. Usually, a flat corporate tax rate is applied to the resulting net income if it is positive.

Table 7: Hypothetical Corporate Income Tax Return

	Amount
Gross Income	50,000
Sales of Goods and Services	35,000
Other Income	15,000
Deductions	47,300
Cost of Goods Sold	35,000
Capital Cost Allowance	7,500
Interest Payments	800
Overhead Expenses	4,000
Net Income	2,700
Net Operating Loss from Prior Years	700
Taxable Income	2,000
Tax Payable	600
Investment Tax Credits	100
Total Tax Payable after Tax Credits	500
Corporate Tax Rate	30%

Source: Author.

[24] For example, to estimate the revenue losses resulting from the tax law provisions with respect to depreciation allowance, the US Department of the Treasury maintains a separate depreciation model.

Estimation Methodology for Tax Expenditures

Revenue losses of corporate tax expenditures can be estimated either by aggregate methods or microsimulation models. In addition, revenue losses can be estimated at the aggregate sector level if sector data are available for components of income and deductions. The key issue in estimating corporate tax expenditure is the determination of final taxable profits. An estimate of the taxable profits would result in an accurate estimate of forgone revenues.

In addition to aggregate and microsimulation models, the revenue impact of tax expenditures can be assessed using the marginal effective tax rate (METR) methodology, explained later.

Special Economic Zones

A special case of corporate tax expenditures is the existence of special economic zones (SEZs) (or free economic zones). SEZs are considered outside the domestic market. Businesses operating in an SEZ are mostly exporting companies. They either purchase their inputs from the domestic market or import them. Their labor force is generally hired from the domestic market with few nonresident employees. In principle, these businesses should be exempt from domestic taxes on goods and services such as VAT and excises, and customs duties. They should be subject to all other taxes. In addition to tax exemptions, they may qualify for investment credits. Thus, their tax treatment is different from that of a regular business operating in the domestic market. It can be considered a special regime. Therefore, it may be necessary to estimate the revenue effects of tax benefits they receive using individual company data collected from the zones by the zone administrations.

Hypothetical Calculation of Each Type of Tax Expenditure

Revenues forgone of corporate tax expenditures can be estimated using aggregate tax data to be compiled by tax administrations. This approach would not provide any information on the sector and size distribution of the benefits. Therefore, for estimations of corporate tax expenditures, microsimulation models using corporate tax returns are preferred.

Aggregate Approach

To estimate the revenues forgone as a result of corporate tax expenditures, data similar to those shown in Table 7 can be collected for the population of all corporate taxpayers. Applying the steps of the tax calculations in a tax return, tax liability with and without the tax expenditure item can be estimated. The model may look similar to the one shown in Table 8. The model tabulates detailed components of income and deductions. In addition, the model includes data on preferential tax rates for businesses operating in SEZs, agricultural firms and extractive industries, and their compliance rates. All income and deductions data are compiled by the tax administration.

To determine the revenue forgone for a tax expenditure item, the adjustment factor would be set to zero. Then, the resulting tax liability would be compared to the baseline tax liability. Table 9 shows the estimate of revenue loss of depreciation allowance. The revenue loss for allowing this deduction is 25.2 million LC.

Table 8: Hypothetical Corporate Income Tax Aggregate Simulation Model

	Baseline	Adjustment to Baseline	Simulation Result
Total Sales:	1,864,007,220		
- Revenue	1,793,818,813	1.0	1,793,818,813
- Revaluation of buildings and non-depreciable assets	9,494,314	1.0	9,494,314
- Interest	338,710	1.0	338,710
- Dividends	36,187	1.0	36,187
- Gains	0	1.0	0
- Gratis property and receipts	415,790	1.0	415,790
- Rent	5,095,178	1.0	5,095,178
- Royalty	0	1.0	0
- Subsidies	3,526,421	1.0	3,526,421
- Income from reduction of reserve funds (banks, insurance, and mining)	854,450	1.0	854,450
- Income from liabilities writing-off	3,940,710	1.0	3,940,710
- Reimbursed losses (previous deductions)	627,330	1.0	627,330
- Other income	45,859,318	1.0	45,859,318
Aggregate Income	**1,864,007,220**		**1,864,007,220**
Adjustment (-):			
- Currency exchange gains	3,412,903	1.0	3,412,903
- Gains from securities transactions (adjusted for inflation)	7,629,365	1.0	7,629,365
- Dividends taxed at source	0	1.0	0
Total Adjustment	**11,042,268**		**11,042,268**
Adjusted Aggregate Income	1,852,964,952		1,852,964,952
Expenditures (-):	1,621,883,815		
- Cost of goods sold	1,162,471,829	1.0	1,162,471,829
- Interest	26,515,687	1.0	26,515,687
- Doubtful debts	129,750,705	1.0	129,750,705
- Reserve fund contribution	48,656,514	1.0	48,656,514
- Research and development expenditures	32,437,676	1.0	32,437,676
- Depreciation and deductions of tangible assets	101,957,229	1.0	101,957,229
- Maintenance (repairs)	29,230,174	1.0	29,230,174
- Insurance	3,159,477	1.0	3,159,477
- Geological exploration expense (for mining and petroleum)	5,247,860	1.0	5,247,860
- Amortization of intangible assets	2,598,195	1.0	2,598,195
- Taxes, penalties	77,260,223	1.0	77,260,223
Total Expenditures	**1,621,883,815**		**1,621,883,815**
Taxable Income	231,081,137		231,081,137

continued on next page

Table 8 *continued*

	Baseline	Adjustment to Baseline	Simulation Result
Deductions (-):			
- Losses carried forward	4,640,834	1.0	4,640,834
- Interest on state securities	3,655,125	1.0	3,655,125
- Charity contributions to nonprofit organizations	445,811	1.0	445,811
- Contributions to fund new equity	1,558	1.0	1,558
- Charity contributions to nonprofit organizations	235,644	1.0	235,644
- Voluntary pension fund contributions	1,212,000	1.0	1,212,000
- Interest on leasing	1,303,275	1.0	1,303,275
Total Deductions	**11,603,625**		**11,603,625**
Taxable Income Adjusted	219,477,512		219,477,512
Share of revenue of enterprises taxed at general rate	94%		94%
Share of revenue of special zones	1%		1%
Share of revenue of land users	2%		2%
Share of revenue of subsurface contracts	3%		3%
Tax Rate (General)	30%		30%
Tax Rate (Special zones)	20%		20%
Tax Rate (Land users)	10%		10%
Tax Rate (Subsurface users)	15%		15%
Tax Compliance (General)	85.0%		85.0%
Tax Compliance (Special zones)	85.0%		85.0%
Tax Compliance (Land users)	85.0%		85.0%
Tax Compliance (Subsurface users)	90.0%		90.0%
Tax (General)	52,608,760		52,608,760
Tax (Special zones)	373,112		373,112
Tax (Land users)	373,112		373,112
Tax (Subsurface users)	888,884		888,884
Total Tax	54,243,867		54,243,867

Source: Author's calculations.

Table 9: Estimate of Revenue Cost of Depreciation Allowance

	Baseline	Adjustment to Baseline	Simulation Result
Total Sales:	1,864,007,220		
- Revenue	1,793,818,813	1.0	1,793,818,813
- Revaluation of buildings and non-depreciable assets	9,494,314	1.0	9,494,314
- Interest	338,710	1.0	338,710
- Dividends	36,187	1.0	36,187
- Gains	0	1.0	0
- Gratis property and receipts	415,790	1.0	415,790
- Rent	5,095,178	1.0	5,095,178
- Royalty	0	1.0	0
- Subsidies	3,526,421	1.0	3,526,421
- Income from reduction of reserve funds (banks, insurance, and mining)	854,450	1.0	854,450
- Income from liabilities writing-off	3,940,710	1.0	3,940,710
- Reimbursed losses (previous deductions)	627,330	1.0	627,330
- Other income	45,859,318	1.0	45,859,318
Aggregate Income	**1,864,007,220**		**1,864,007,220**
Adjustment (-):			
- Currency exchange gains	3,412,903	1.0	3,412,903
- Gains from securities transactions (adjusted for inflation)	7,629,365	1.0	7,629,365
- Dividends taxed at source	0	1.0	0
Total Adjustment	**11,042,268**		**11,042,268**
Adjusted Aggregate Income	1,852,964,952		1,852,964,952
Expenditures (-):	1,621,883,815		
- Cost of goods sold	1,162,471,829	1.0	1,162,471,829
- Interest	26,515,687	1.0	26,515,687
- Doubtful debts	129,750,705	1.0	129,750,705
- Reserve fund contribution	48,656,514	1.0	48,656,514
- Research and development expenditures	32,437,676	1.0	32,437,676
- Depreciation and deductions of tangible assets	101,957,229	0.0	0
- Maintenance (repairs)	29,230,174	1.0	29,230,174
- Insurance	3,159,477	1.0	3,159,477
- Geological exploration expense (for mining and petroleum)	5,247,860	1.0	5,247,860
- Amortization of intangible assets	2,598,195	1.0	2,598,195
- Taxes, penalties	77,260,223	1.0	77,260,223
Total Expenditures	**1,621,883,815**		**1,519,926,586**
Taxable Income	231,081,137		333,038,366

continued on next page

Table 9 *continued*

	Baseline	Adjustment to Baseline	Simulation Result
Deductions (-):			
- Losses carried forward	4,640,834	1.0	4,640,834
- Interest on state securities	3,655,125	1.0	3,655,125
- Charity contributions to nonprofit organizations	445,811	1.0	445,811
- Contributions to fund new equity	1,558	1.0	1,558
- Charity contributions to nonprofit organizations	235,644	1.0	235,644
- Voluntary pension fund contributions	1,212,000	1.0	1,212,000
- Interest on leasing	1,303,275	1.0	1,303,275
Total Deductions	**11,603,625**		**11,603,625**
Taxable Income Adjusted	**219,477,512**		**321,434,741**
Share of revenue of enterprises taxed at general rate	94%		94%
Share of revenue of special zones	1%		1%
Share of revenue of land users	2%		2%
Share of revenue of subsurface contracts	3%		3%
Tax Rate (General)	30%		30%
Tax Rate (Special zones)	20%		20%
Tax Rate (Land users)	10%		10%
Tax Rate (Subsurface users)	15%		15%
Tax Compliance (General)	85.0%		85.0%
Tax Compliance (Special zones)	85.0%		85.0%
Tax Compliance (Land users)	85.0%		85.0%
Tax Compliance (Subsurface users)	90.0%		90.0%
Tax (General)	52,608,760		77,047,907
Tax (Special zones)	373,112		546,439
Tax (Land users)	373,112		546,439
Tax (Subsurface users)	888,884		1,301,811
Total Tax	**54,243,867**		**79,442,596**

Source: Author's calculations.

Microsimulation Model

The corporate microsimulation would use a sample of corporate tax returns or the returns of all the corporate taxpayers. The model produces the revenue and distributional impacts of various policy changes such as changes in tax rates, tax incentives, and changes in the rules of deductible expenses such as depreciation allowances. A hypothetical corporate microsimulation model would include a parameter template, a data template where the tax calculator calculates the tax liability with new parameter values, and a template that shows the resulting change in tax liabilities by industry. Table 10 shows the parameter template of a microsimulation model with tax rates, depreciation rates, and investment credits.

Table 10: Parameter Template of a Corporate Microsimulation Model

TOTAL TAXES PAID			
BASE CASE	7,336,167,651		
REFORM	7,336,167,651		
IMPACT	–	0.0%	

BASE CASE			SIMULATION		
Tax and Deduction Rates		**Rate**	**Tax and Deduction Rates**		**Rate**
P1TX	Basic CIT rate	28%	P1TX	Basic CIT rate	28%
SBD	SBD rate	16%	SBD	SBD rate	16%
MPPD	MPPD rate	7%	MPPD	MPPD rate	7%
Capital Cost Allowance Rates			**Capital Cost Allowance Rates**		
CCA		**Rate**	**CCA**		**Rate**
CCA1		20%	CCA1		20%
CCA2		50%	CCA2		50%
CCA3		0%	CCA3		0%
Investment Tax Credit Rates		**Rate**	**Investment Tax Credit Rates**		**Rate**
ITC		20%	ITC		20%

P1TX: basic corporate income tax
SBD: small business deduction
MPPD: manufacturing and processing deduction
CCA: capital cost allowance (tax depreciation allowance)
ITC: investment tax credit

Source: Author's compilation.

The data are obtained from taxpayer returns. The total number of taxpayers is 17,699. The sample size is 300 observations, which is a sampling rate of 1.7%. Table 11 shows the taxpayer data from each selected sample member. Each line includes the industry the taxpayer belongs to, its asset size, and financial data required to calculate the tax liability. The tax calculator calculates the tax liability of the taxpayer under a baseline scenario, which is the current law and an alternative scenario.

The output of the simulation is summarized in a table to observe the change in tax liability easily. Table 12 shows the output of the simulations by industry.

The total revenue loss, as a result of providing an investment credit, is 387.3 million or 5.3% of total tax liabilities. It is also possible to demonstrate the revenue forgone by size of corporations.

Table 11: Taxpayer Data for the Corporate Microsimulation Model

(Part 1)

Base Population		
No. of Corporations	17,699	300
Total Tax Liability (000)	7,336,168	1.70%

No	Weight (# Corps)	Industry	Size Code	Size	Assets	Net Income Financial	Book Depreciation	Book Tax
1	97	13. Mining	2	Small	4,439	925,068	611	0
2	87	13. Mining	6	Medium	4,879,565	368,957	114,686	0
3	8	08. Retail Trade	8	Large	11,232,533	22,394,934	2,642,027	3,737,367
4	8	13. Mining	8	Large	3,449,357	22,901,672	3,157,822	3,883,313
5	84	12. Oil, Gas	2	Small	1,027,829	1,101,556	65,224	0
6	11	02. Manufacturing	3	Small	496,620	1,724,478	124,064	0
7	22	11. Services	3	Small	2,366,139	-565,877	145,097	0
8	8	04. Transport, Storg	8	Large	14,119,023	25,480,760	1,443,863	2,788,557
9	95	06. Publ Utilities	5	Medium	68,064	-578,634	227,243	0
10	8	08. Retail Trade	7	Large	26,509,397	-1,680,248	593,212	0
11	81	07. Wholesale Trade	5	Medium	1,499,543	1,348,846	216,073	0
12	30	04. Transport, Storg	2	Small	34,900	1,307,332	11,651	0

(Part 2)

No	Weight (# Corps)	Industry	Capital Cost Allowance (Tax Depreciation)	Net Income (Tax)	Donations	Loss	Manufacturing Income	Taxable Income
1	97	13. Mining	111	925,568	1,452	3,234	0	920,882
2	87	13. Mining	147,193	336,450	0	5,525	0	330,926
3	8	08. Retail Trade	224,651	28,549,677	0	1,341,498	0	27,208,180
4	8	13. Mining	68,987	29,873,820	1,595	1,742,571	0	28,129,654
5	84	12. Oil, Gas	32,893	1,133,887	292	21,472	0	1,112,123
6	11	02. Manufacturing	11,871	1,836,671	0	81,656	78,472	1,755,015
7	22	11. Services	78,488	-499,269	88	0	0	0
8	8	04. Transport, Storg	435,914	29,277,266	0	1,737,731	0	27,539,535
9	95	06. Publ Utilities	1,632	-353,022	1,359	0	0	0
10	8	08. Retail Trade	858,684	-1,945,721	2,305	0	0	0
11	81	07. Wholesale Trade	29,991	1,534,928	0	125,387	0	1,409,542
12	30	04. Transport, Storg	882	1,318,101	1,108	75,859	0	1,241,134

Source: Author's calculations.

Table 12: **Output of Repealing Investment Tax Credit**

Industry	Size Sum of CIT (simulation) Large	Medium	Small	Size Sum of CIT (base) Large	Medium	Small
01. Agr. Forestry, Fishing	106,852,646		34,075,870	95,939,555		34,075,870
02. Manufacturing	333,559,019	67,176,512	56,468,041	311,221,766	48,619,345	55,797,417
03. Construction	161,646,164	157,449,347	98,883,975	158,941,485	144,487,280	89,256,762
04. Transport, Storg	178,329,119	313,049,657	128,199,325	173,330,754	259,482,164	119,647,376
05. Communication	88,907,958	98,281,354	324,176,099	88,891,309	94,302,578	306,736,641
06. Publ Utilities	295,437,574	206,877,092	125,858,810	295,437,574	199,012,323	118,435,347
07. Wholesale Trade	252,203,170	383,965,542	115,892,077	250,385,494	376,567,704	112,168,558
08. Retail Trade	343,160,771	281,052,119	39,701,384	335,949,128	250,287,218	34,879,754
09. Dep-Acc Inst	181,756,094	383,807,870	80,196,438	165,050,799	380,624,661	79,203,578
10. Other Finance	178,899,344	263,923,529	188,371,412	177,528,809	233,147,814	173,451,298
11. Services	220,638,485	224,137,678	91,776,310	216,889,919	205,625,138	89,487,682
12. Oil, Gas	164,986,237	330,223,238	164,966,006	164,986,237	323,838,359	164,964,988
13. Mining	273,340,422	93,227,636	206,945,025	262,714,133	69,280,295	196,775,959
14. Other	186,592,856	258,898,916	39,543,467	186,592,856	257,011,639	35,140,090
Grand Total	2,966,309,857	3,062,070,490	1,695,054,238	2,883,859,817	2,842,286,515	1,610,021,318
Total Taxes Paid						
Base Case		7,336,167,651				
Simulation		7,723,434,586				
Impact		387,266,935				

CIT = corporate income tax.
Source: Author's calculations.

Marginal Effective Tax Rate

Marginal effective tax rates (METRs) are designed to measure the tax benefits for investment, considering the effects income stream of the project over its lifetime. The calculation measures the impact of taxes on a marginal investment project. Comparing the METR between a benchmark tax system and the one without the tax expenditures provides an estimate of the extent of the tax expenditures in terms of an effective tax rate. In some cases where the benefits are distributed over a long period, neither the aggregate model nor the microsimulation model can capture the revenue effect of tax expenditures. Therefore, METR calculations are necessary for estimating the revenue effects of these tax benefits, such as tax holidays, various forms of depreciation allowances, investment deductions, and tax benefits of alternative financing methods. Even though tax expenditures in the form of investment tax incentives may induce investors to invest different than otherwise determined by market conditions, the outcome of investments may be different than the anticipated economic impact. Therefore, investment tax incentives may sometimes result in resource misallocation and inefficiency (Abbas et al.).

METR on capital calculates an effective tax rate on capital that considers all the features of the tax provisions, such as the statutory tax rates, deductions, depreciation, credits, tax holidays, and other benefits over the lifetime of the investment. In calculating the effective tax rate, it also includes borrowing costs and the inflation rate. It can also include features of individual income taxes when calculating the after-tax returns. METRs can be calculated for industries or asset types separately. METRs are sensitive to the assumptions about inflation, cost of borrowing, and share of financing by debt or equity. The METR methodology is described in detail in Appendix 1.

A hypothetical METR model is demonstrated and its parameters are shown in Table 13. It will include parameters such as the inflation rate, interest rate, share of the investment financed by debt, and depreciation rates.

Table 13: Hypothetical Marginal Effective Tax Rate Model Parameters

A. General input data			
	Baseline (%)	**Simulation (%)**	
$\rho-\pi$	5.0	5.0	Fixed real required after-corporate tax rate of return on equity
rb	3.0	3.0	Fixed real interest rate on bonds
Π	2.0	2.0	Inflation rate
P	7.0	7.0	Nominal required after-corporate tax rate of return, where $\rho = (\rho-\pi)+\pi$
I	5.0	5.0	Interest rate (nominal) = $rb+\pi$
B	40.0	40.0	Debt/asset ratio (average)
RN	4.2	4.2	Fixed real required after-corporate tax rate of return on equity and debt, $RN = \beta^*i+(1-\beta)^*\rho-\pi$
General economic depreciation rates (δ)			
buildings 1	5.0	5.0	Declining-balance equivalent of straight-line depreciation
buildings 2	7.0	7.0	Declining-balance equivalent of straight-line depreciation
machinery 1	10.0	10.0	Declining balance
machinery 2	20.0	20.0	Declining balance
machinery 3	90.0	90.0	Declining balance
machinery 4	30.0	30.0	Declining balance
Tax depreciation rates (α)			
CCA buildings 1	6.0	6.0	Declining balance equivalent of straight-line depreciation
CCA buildings 2	8.0	8.0	Declining balance equivalent of straight-line depreciation
CCA machinery 1	15.0	15.0	Declining balance
CCA machinery 2	25.0	25.0	Declining balance
CCA machinery 3	100.0	100.0	Declining balance
CCA machinery 4	40.0	40.0	Declining balance
CIT rate			
U	35.0	35.0	Statutory corporate income tax rate (general rate)
E. Investment tax credit (ξ)	10.0	0	

CCA = capital cost allowance, CIT = corporate income tax.

Source: Author's calculations.

In this case, tax expenditure items are depreciation allowances, investment tax credits, and tax treatment of financing methods. All these tax expenditure items relate to investments spread over several years. Therefore, it is necessary to estimate the revenue loss over the lifetime of the investment. To determine the revenue loss of an investment tax credit of 10% on the value of machinery investments in the manufacturing industry, the METR model calculates effective tax rate (the difference between the rate of return before and after taxes) for the base case that includes the investment tax credit and for the simulation without the investment tax credit. The model inputs, including the investment credits in the manufacturing industry, are shown in Table 14.

The simulation results in Table 15 show that the primary beneficiary of the incentive is the manufacturing industry. Further, the incentive is targeted for investments in machinery. Negative METRs are sometimes possible.[25] A negative METR after the introduction of a tax benefit implies that, over the lifetime of the investment, tax expenditures are subsidies financing the project.[26] Therefore, METR estimates should be considered as guidance for policy designers when they provide investment incentives.

Table 14: Hypothetical Marginal Effective Tax Rate Model—Inputs

C. Industry tax rates and financing weights								
	Agriculture and Fishing	**Electrical Power, Gas and Water**	**Construction**	**Manufacturing**	**Wholesale Trade**	**Retail Trade**	**Transportation and Storage**	**Communications**
u	0.350	0.350	0.350	0.350	0.350	0.350	0.350	0.350
β	0.400	0.400	0.400	0.400	0.400	0.400	0.400	0.400
D. Financing cost and required after-corporate-tax rate of return								
	Agriculture and Fishing	Electrical Power, Gas and Water	Construction	Manufacturing	Wholesale Trade	Retail Trade	Transportation and Storage	Communications
R	0.055	0.055	0.055	0.055	0.055	0.055	0.055	0.055
R-π	0.035	0.035	0.035	0.035	0.035	0.035	0.035	0.035
E. Investment tax credit (ξ)								
	Agriculture and Fishing	**Electrical Power, Gas and Water**	**Construction**	**Manufacturing**	**Wholesale Trade**	**Retail Trade**	**Transportation and Storage**	**Communications**
Buildings 1	0.000	0.000	0.000	0.000	0.000	0.000	0.000	0.000
Buildings 2	0.000	0.000	0.000	0.000	0.000	0.000	0.000	0.000
Machinery 1	0.000	0.000	0.000	0.000	0.000	0.000	0.000	0.000
Machinery 2	0.000	0.000	0.000	0.000	0.000	0.000	0.000	0.000
Machinery 3	0.000	0.000	0.000	0.000	0.000	0.000	0.000	0.000
Machinery 4	0.000	0.000	0.000	0.000	0.000	0.000	0.000	0.000
Land	0.000	0.000	0.000	0.000	0.000	0.000	0.000	0.000
Inventory	0.000	0.000	0.000	0.000	0.000	0.000	0.000	0.000

Source: Author's calculations.

[25] Sometimes a combination of interest expenses and high depreciation allowances may result in negative METRs.

[26] It should be noted that a negative METR before the introduction of any tax benefit is an indication that the project is not financially viable because it has negative profits.

Table 15: Simulation Results of Repealing the Investment Tax Credit

Baseline

I. Marginal effective tax rate METR=(RG-RN)/RG

	Agriculture and Fishing	Electrical Power, Gas and Water	Construction	Manufacturing	Wholesale Trade	Retail Trade	Transportation and Storage	Communications	Total Sectors
Buildings	0.271	0.271	0.271	0.271	0.271	0.271	0.271	0.271	0.271
Machinery	0.266	0.266	0.266	−0.749	0.266	0.266	0.266	0.266	0.106
Land	0.220	0.220	0.220	0.220	0.220	0.220	0.220	0.220	0.220
Inventory	0.220	0.220	0.220	0.220	0.220	0.220	0.220	0.220	0.220
Aggregate	0.253	0.263	0.249	−0.041	0.242	0.246	0.263	0.265	0.188

Simulation

I. Marginal effective tax rate METR=(RG-RN)/RG

	Agriculture and Fishing	Electrical Power, Gas and Water	Construction	Manufacturing	Wholesale Trade	Retail Trade	Transportation and Storage	Communications	Total Sectors
Buildings	0.271	0.271	0.271	0.271	0.271	0.271	0.271	0.271	0.271
Machinery	0.266	0.266	0.266	0.266	0.266	0.266	0.266	0.266	0.266
Land	0.220	0.220	0.220	0.220	0.220	0.220	0.220	0.220	0.220
Inventory	0.220	0.220	0.220	0.220	0.220	0.220	0.220	0.220	0.220
Aggregate	0.253	0.263	0.249	0.257	0.242	0.246	0.263	0.265	0.258
Diff	0.000	0.000	0.000	0.000	0.000	0.000	0.000	0.000	0.000
	0.000	0.000	0.000	1.015	0.000	0.000	0.000	0.000	0.160
	0.000	0.000	0.000	0.000	0.000	0.000	0.000	0.000	0.000
	0.000	0.000	0.000	0.000	0.000	0.000	0.000	0.000	0.000
	0.000	0.000	0.000	0.298	0.000	0.000	0.000	0.000	0.070

Source: Author's calculations.

Discussion of Data Sources

For aggregate estimates like the one shown in Table 10, external sources such as national accounts or business surveys are not sufficient for constructing a detailed model. The components of income and deductions have to be obtained from tax administration sources. Tax administrations can provide summary statistics on the components of income and deductions.

The data requirement of corporate microsimulation models is burdensome, and a file containing data on each taxpayer needs to be developed with cooperation from the tax administration. In Table 10, basic components of income and deductions are shown to construct the corporate microsimulation database. Taxpayer data for the most recent complete year would be sufficient. However, if there are loss carryforwards, then a stock of these losses should be kept and used assuming tax minimization. The data can be aged to estimate revenues forgone in the future years.

Data for METR estimates can be collected from external sources. The most important component is the capital stock by industry. Capital stock data must be broken down by type of assets such as buildings, machinery, transport equipment, and office equipment. Statistical agencies provide such studies on the size and distribution of capital stock.[27]

Value-Added Tax

Generally Accepted Tax Expenditures Under Value-Added Tax

The main purpose of value-added tax (VAT) is to raise revenue in a predictable and efficient manner. Because it has a stable base which is the final consumption, it provides a stable revenue source not effected from economic fluctuations. Unlike the excises that aim to change the behavior of consumers for health or environmental reasons, VAT does not alter the economic decisions of individuals. Since it is evenly applied to both locally produced and imported goods, it does not alter trade flows. Also, VAT does not play a role like income tax or the tax on profits in influencing income distribution or investment decisions by firms. Therefore, an ideal VAT taxes all goods and services uniformly based on the destination principle.

Exemptions from VAT should be limited to those activities that are technically difficult, such as financial services where the value added is based on the intermediation and those where the administrative costs would be higher than the revenue yield. Therefore, there should be a threshold for small businesses and farmers. There should also be no or minimal tax expenditures applicable to the VAT system because these tax expenditures would not generally serve a well-defined objective. VAT tax expenditures are in the form of a lower VAT rate than the standard rate, exempting certain goods and services from VAT and zero rate applied to selected goods and services. These tax benefits are provided on local and imported goods and services.

The components of a VAT system are as follows:

Zero rating: Trade is taxed on a destination basis (i.e., where goods are consumed). Therefore, exports are zero rated.

Input credits for capital goods: VAT charged on capital goods can be credited in full immediately.

Number of rates: A single VAT rate for all goods and services with a zero rate for exports is recommended; there may be one more rate, usually at a reduced rate, for basic goods and services.

Threshold: It is common to have a threshold, usually based on turnover, below which businesses need not file for VAT.

Exemptions: Certain services, principally public health and education, and non-fee financial services, are often exempt from the VAT for policy and practical reasons. However, nonstandard exemptions exist in practice, particularly, including imports and supplies related to diplomats, nongovernment organizations, donor-funded projects, and incentives provided under investment laws.

---

[27] The common methodology used by statistics agencies in calculating the capital stock is the perpetual inventory method on investment expenditures. This is also supplemented by business surveys on investments.

Broadly, seven categories are considered for exemption:[28]

- agricultural products and key agricultural inputs;
- fuels;
- passenger transport;
- non-fee financial services;
- cultural and other merit items (such as books and newspapers, and noncommercial activities of religious organizations);
- aid-financed activities; and
- capital goods (essentially imported capital goods).

However, it should be noted that VAT exemptions do not necessarily imply revenue losses and there are circumstances in which they may even boost revenue. This does not mean, however, that they do no harm. On the contrary, they are harmful for distorting relative prices, thus introducing inefficiency in the economy, and may promote inequity if there is revenue forgone and the benefits accrue in most part to high-income households, while the lower revenue level prevents the government from spending in actions and programs targeted to the poorer population.

The hypothetical transactions presented in Table 16 show several cases of VAT exemptions. A producer uses chicks, corn, and other inputs to raise chickens that are sold to a manufacturer. The manufacturer freezes the chicken meat using electric power as an input and sells frozen chicken meat to a market who sells to final consumers. The VAT is charged on these transactions at 10%. To simplify the explanation, it is assumed that, in all cases, the consumer pays 100 for the chicken, the market pays 90, and the manufacturer 70 (plus VAT if there is not an exemption). In "total tax," the numbers in parentheses are the taxes that the input suppliers collect and pay to the tax administration. The other numbers are the net liabilities of the producer, the manufacturer, and the market. The column "Taxes on all transactions" is the standard VAT piecemeal collection. It is assumed that no inputs are necessary to produce chicks, corn, electric power, and the other inputs used to raise chickens.

The effects of exemptions on the revenue depend on the point of the production and commercialization chain where the exemption applies. If the first transaction of a production and commercialization chain is exempt, like in the case "Exemption for corn," total tax is the same as in the standard case. The revenue forgone due to the exemption is recovered when the producer presents the VAT return and pays the tax, since the input VAT credit is smaller.

The situation is different if the exemption is for a transaction in the middle of the production and commercialization chain. The column "Exemption for producer" shows that, in this case, "total tax" increases from 10 to 16. This happens because the exemption breaks the debit–credit chain of VAT. The information about taxation of inputs previously used is lost, and the value of the inputs (equals to the value added to chicken up to the exemption) is taxed twice. The revenue will increase more if the government grants an exemption to the manufacturer as well (column "Exemption for producer and manufacturer"). It would increase further if the manufacturer, but not the producer, is contemplated with an exemption (case not shown) because the value added by the producer (10), which was exempt in the previous case, would also be taxed twice.

[28] See Ebrill et al. (2001).

Table 16: Effect of Value-Added Tax Exemptions—A Hypothetical Example

Production Unit	Product	Values	Taxes Paid: Taxes on All Transactions	Taxes Paid: Exemption for Corn	Taxes Paid: Exemption for Producer	Taxes Paid: Exemption for Producer and Manufacturer
Producer	Chick	10	1	1	1	1
	Corn	40	4	Exempt	4	4
	Other inputs	10	1	1	1	1
	Sells chicken	70	7-1-4-1=1	7-1-1=5	Exempt	Exempt
Manufacturer	Buys chicken	70	7	7	0	0
	Electric power	10	1	1	1	1
	Sells frozen chicken	90	9-7-1=1	9-7-1=1	9-1=8	Exempt
Market	Purchases	90	9	9	9	0
	Sells	100	10-9 = 1	10-9=1	10-9=1	10-0=10
Tax rate = 10%	Total tax		(1+4+1+1)+1+1+1=10	(1+1+1)+5+1+1 =10	(1+4+1+1)+0+8+1 =16	(1+4+1+1)+0+0+10=17

Production Unit	Product	Values	Taxes Paid: Exemption for Sale to Consumer	Taxes Paid: Exemption for Manufacturer and Market	Taxes Paid: Exemption for Producer, Manufacturer, and Market	Taxes Paid: Exemption for the Three on Sales and Purchases
Producer	Chick	10	1	1	1	Exempt
	Corn	40	4	4	4	Exempt
	Other inputs	10	1	1	1	Exempt
	Sells chicken	70	7-1-4-1=1	7-1-4-1=1	Exempt	Exempt
Manufacturer	Buys chicken	70	7	7	0	0
	Electric power	10	1	1	1	Exempt
	Sells frozen chicken	90	9-7-1=1	Exempt	Exempt	Exempt
Market	Purchases	90	9	0	0	0
	Sells	100	Exempt	Exempt	Exempt	Exempt
Tax rate = 10%	Total tax		(1+4+1+1)+1+1+0=9	(1+4+1+1)+1+0+0 = 8	(1+4+1+1) = 7	0

Source: Author's calculations.

The second half of the table shows cases in which the exemption would create a tax expenditure. This happens if the government grants an exemption at the end of the production and commercialization chain. However, the tax expenditure corresponds only to the tax on the value added by the market (column "Exemption for the sale to consumer"). If the government grants the exemption also to the manufacturer, the tax expenditure increases, and increases further if exemption is granted to the producer as well. Nevertheless, in all these cases, the tax expenditures are less than the full amount of the tax. The tax expenditure will be equal to the amount of the total tax on chicken only if the purchases of inputs by the producer and the manufacturer are also exempt (column "Exemption for the three on sales and purchases"). Alternatively, the government would forgo the full amount of the tax if the sales of the three agents were zero rated.

Both subjective exemptions and zero-rated transactions pose difficult problems for the tax administration.[29] If the government grants an exemption to the supplies of corn to the chicken producer but not to other customers, it provides an opportunity for fraud that is difficult to control. The corn supplier may issue an invoice to the chicken producer but deliver the corn to another customer, giving rise to a chain of evasion. Zero-rating domestic transactions meant for specific purchasers create the same problem and a second one—an increase in the number of cases and amounts of VAT refunds.[30] Two important implications follow: first, VAT exemptions should not be subjective, and second, domestic transactions should not be zero rated.

Estimation Methodology for Tax Expenditures

There are three commonly practiced approaches to estimate the VAT base and forgone revenues: aggregate national account approach/sector national account approach, household consumption survey approach, and input–output (I–O) table approach. The important step in estimating the revenues forgone from VAT-related tax expenditures is the determination of the tax base.[31]

Aggregate National Account Approach

Under the aggregate national account approach, the gross domestic product (GDP) is adjusted to arrive at a VAT base consistent with a destination-based VAT. Adjustments include trade balance, which is the difference between exports and imports, capital formation (because investment goods are not taxed), exemptions and cascading resulting from the sale of exempt goods, government expenditures on wages and salaries, exemption threshold, and compliance rates.[32] This approach provides a quick estimation of the expected VAT liability where distributional and sector tax burden are not considered to be an issue.

The VAT base under this approach is calculated as follows:

GDP = Consumption + Gross capital formation + Government expenditures + Exports - Imports

Subtract:

- trade balance (i.e., exports–imports)
- gross capital formation
- wages and salaries in government sector
- private and government expenditures abroad
- zero-rated consumption expenditures
- exempt consumption expenditures
- imputed rents for owner-occupied dwellings

---

29 Subjective exemptions are those that are granted to a particular buyer of a good or service rather than to the good or service itself (objective exemptions).

30 This is like the so-called "carousel fraud," which creates serious problems for the administrations of European Union countries and Brazilian states. For example, some countries report problems of control in transactions between domestic companies and those that are residents of free economic zones (FEZs), despite the ring-fencing of the FEZs. Carousel trade refers to the practice of importing goods from a country where they are not subject to VAT, selling them with VAT added, then deliberately not paying the VAT. This type of fraud happens in European Union countries.

31 See Hutton (2015).

32 See Le (2007).

Add:

- business inputs purchased by exempt sectors
- new residential construction (if subject to tax)[33]

The resulting GDP, after netting out doubly counted items and new additions, becomes a close proxy to the actual VAT base.

Household Survey Approach

In principle, VAT is imposed ultimately on the final consumption of goods and services. Therefore, household expenditure surveys can be used to determine the consumption expenditures subject to VAT. Then, an effective VAT rate can be applied to the consumption expenditures subject to VAT.[34]

Input-Output Simulation Model Approach

The I–O simulation model is applied to a typical consumption-based VAT base, which excludes capital goods and intermediate inputs from the VAT base through a credit-invoice mechanism. The I–O simulation model requires adjustments similar to the ones outlined for the national account approach for estimating VAT revenue and expenditures.

As in the case of aggregate approaches, further adjustments have to be made to account for the impact of exemptions, zero rating, and a VAT threshold. Annual national statistics and business and household consumption surveys can be used as supplementary data sources for necessary assumptions for all three modeling approaches.

Overall, the three different approaches should generate consistent results of projected VAT revenues and VAT compliance rate. As I–O tables generally provide the most detailed accounting of the supply and use of intermediate goods and services, and final consumption expenditures in an economy, the I–O modeling of VAT can be considered the best approach to estimate the disaggregate impact of tax expenditures on the collection and compliance at commodity level.

The analysis of the impact of VAT tax expenditure could focus on income distribution and consumption choices. The distributional effects of VAT tax expenditures include two aspects: (i) to assess the impact on the broad distribution of overall effects of the current VAT system, and (ii) to examine the effectiveness of specific reduced rates/exemptions on the distribution of income, as well as its effects on consumption, investment, and growth for special zones, industry, or sectors.

[33] Sales of new residential construction is generally considered taxable, therefore, included in the benchmark.

[34] Effective VAT rate = VAT collections$_{(t-1)}$/Consumption expenditures subject to VAT. VAT collections reflect all exemptions and zero ratings, while consumption expenditures include exempt and zero-rated goods and service. Therefore, an effective tax rate is appropriate.

Table 17: Estimation of Effect of Value-Added Tax Exemptions—A Hypothetical Example

The Base of Consumption-VAT = $GDP - G^{w} - I = C + G_{c} + (X - M)$ + *Adjustments*

		($ million)	As Share of GDP (%)
GDP		879.0	
Adjustments			
(-)	Net exports	-404.0	-46.0
	Exports	155.0	17.6
	Imports	559.0	63.6
Capital Formation			
(-)	Gross capital formation	203.1	23.1
(+)	Capital formation in residential buildings	79.1	9.0
(-)	Capital formation of exempt sectors		
Exempt Industries			
(-)	Value added of exempt industries (finance, insurance, agriculture)	153.7	17.5
(-)	Indirect taxes paid by exempt sectors		
(+)	Sales of exempt industries to taxable industries	18.5	2.1
(+)	Taxable inputs of exportable agriculture	17.3	2.0
Government			
(-)	Expenditure on wages and salaries	115.3	13.1
(-)	Other nontaxable expenditures (transfers, capital acquisition)	126.9	14.4
Private	**(Households)**		
(-)	Exempt expenditures (rent, financial, health, education)	170.0	19.3
(+)	Taxed inputs of exempt expenditures	87.7	10.0
(-)	Expenditures abroad by residents		
Exemption Threshold			
(-)	Sales of firms below threshold	8.8	1.0
(+)	Taxed inputs by firms below threshold	4.4	0.5
Tax Adjustment			0.0
(-)	**GST to be replaced by VAT**	**38.0**	**4.3**
Noncompliance			
(-)	Compliance rate - Domestic		
	Compliance rate - Imports		
(=)	**Potential VAT Base**	**674.2**	**76.7**
	Potential VAT Base - Imports	**396.9**	**45.2**
	Potential VAT Base - Domestic	**277.3**	**31.6**
	Potential VAT Base Adjusted for Compliance	**535.6**	**60.9**
	Tax Base as a Percentage of GDP	61%	0.1
	VAT Rate		0.0
	Potential VAT Revenue	**47.2**	**5.4**

GDP = gross domestic product, GST = goods and services tax, VAT = value-added tax.
Source: Author's calculations.

Hypothetical Calculation of Each Type of Tax Expenditure

Aggregate National Account Approach

Revenue loss estimates resulting from tax benefits under the VAT system can be estimated starting with the expenditure national account as described above. Table 17 demonstrates the use of national accounts in estimating the revenue impact of tax expenditures.

To estimate the revenue forgone under each exempt item, the respective lines marked with a negative sign in column 1 have to be adjusted by removing the exempt amount. Then, the VAT revenue would be calculated applying the VAT rate to the resulting tax base. In the case of a preferential VAT rate for a given industry, the VAT rate has to be adjusted to reflect the reduced rate.[35] As can be observed, this approach is an imprecise method of estimating the revenue losses of VAT tax expenditures.

Household Survey Approach

To estimate the revenues forgone using the household survey data, the effective VAT rate has to be calculated. The VAT effective rate can be calculated as follows:

$$VATR_{effective} = \frac{VAT\ collections}{Consumption\ expenditure\ subject\ to VAT}$$

This rate would be applied to the VAT-exempt consumption expenditure obtained from the household income and expenditure survey. Household expenditure surveys are reported as average household expenditures. Therefore, the average expenditure of the tax-exempt item has to be multiplied by the number of households in order to obtain the total revenue forgone. The revenue estimate can be calculated as follows:

$$\begin{gathered} Revenue\ Forgone = Avg.\ household\ consumption * Share\ of\ the\ exempt\ item \\ * Number\ of\ households * Effective\ VAT\ rate\ on\ exempt\ consumption \end{gathered}$$

Input–Output Simulation Model Approach

The I–O model uses a table of inter-industry transactions and a table of final demand compiled by national statistics agencies. The rows represent sales to other industries and final demand that includes households, government, and exports (the rest of the world) as shown in Table 18. The columns represent the purchases of inputs of each industry from other industries, labor and capital, and imports. Thus, sales minus purchases by industry provides a detailed prediction of the VAT base.

[35] The new VAT rate would be the weighted average of the two rates. The VAT rate would be

$$t_{VAT} = w_{standard}\, t_{standard} + w_{reduced}\, t_{reduced}$$

where $w_{standard}$ is the share of goods and services in total consumption subject to the standard VAT rate and $w_{reduced}$ is the share of goods and services in total consumption subject to the reduced rate.

Table 18: The Structure of an Input–Output Table

Industry	1 2 n	Intermediate Demand	Final Demand	Total Output
1 2 n	Intermediate Use (X_{ij})	($\Sigma_j X_i$)	(Y_j)	(X_i)
Intermediate Consumption	($\Sigma_j X_i$)			
Value Added	(VA_j)			
Imports	(M_j)			
Total Resources	(X_j)			

Source: Author's representation.

Consider the expenditure components of GDP as follows. These are the components of final demand (final sales) listed in the following table.

C	Consumption	100
I	Investment	10
G	Government	20
X	Exports	29
M	Imports	-33
GDP	Gross domestic product	126

These final sales to the ultimate users were produced by the industries listed in the following table.

	C	I	G	X	M	Total
Raw materials	0	0	0	10	-5	5
Food	30	0	3	5	-3	35
Clothing	10	0	1	2	-5	8
Other goods	40	10	8	12	-20	50
Other services	20	0	4	0	0	24
Value added	0	0	4	0	0	4
Total	100	10	20	29	-33	126

These final sales were produced by sales and purchases between the industries as shown in the following table.

	Raw Materials Industry	Food Industry	Clothing Industry	Other Goods Industry	Other Services Industry	Total
Raw materials	0	10	2	20	0	32
Food	0	0	0	0	0	0
Clothing	0	0	0	0	0	0
Other goods	0	5	2	23	10	40
Other services	0	5	2	27	0	34
Value added	37	15	2	20	48	122
Total	37	35	8	90	58	228

These three tables form the I–O table which is the basis of the simulation model used in estimating revenues forgone under VAT tax expenditures. An I–O-based VAT simulation model would consist of a parameter file that includes VAT rates, exemption shares, and share of zero-rated goods and services. Table 19 shows the parameter template. Parameters are marked in blue, and they can be changed to estimate revenue forgone due to a tax expenditure such as a reduced rate or an exemption. The database is a 32-industry I–O table that shows the inter-industry sales and purchases, and final sales. The rows of the I–O table include sales of goods and services of industries to other industries and final demand that can be used in calculating the output VAT. The columns include purchases of industries from other industries that can be used in calculating input VAT. However, the inter-industry sales and purchases have to be adjusted for purchases and sales of exempt goods similar to the adjustments shown in Table 17. There may be zero-rated sales as well. These adjustments are parameterized for each industry in the parameter template (Table 19).

Table 19: Parameter Template of the Input–Output Model

Industries	Tax Rate for Sales	Gross Domestic Output (incl. imports)	Imports	Exempt Imports	Exports	Zero-Rated Export	Exempt Sales	Zero-Rated Sales
		6,752,760	1,283,051		1,529,352			
Agriculture, hunting, and forestry	10%	6%	1%	0%	9%	100%	0%	0%
Fishing, fish breeding	20%	0%	0%	0%	0%	100%	0%	0%
Mining		15%	3%		38%			
Manufacturing		32%	77%		39%			
Production and distribution of electricity, gas, and water	20%	3%	3%	0%	0%	100%	0%	0%
Construction	20%	6%	6%	0%	0%	100%	0%	0%
Trade, repair of motor vehicles and personal and household goods	20%	11%	0%	0%	0%	100%	0%	0%
Hotels and restaurants	20%	1%	2%	0%	2%	100%	0%	0%
Transport	20%	9%	5%	0%	5%	100%	0%	0%
Post and communication	20%	1%	0%	0%	0%	100%	0%	0%
Financial activities	0%	2%	1%	100%	0%	100%	100%	0%
Real estate activities, lease, and services rendered to enterprises	20%	7%	0%	0%	5%	100%	0%	0%
Government administration	0%	2%	0%	100%	1%	100%	100%	0%
Education	0%	2%	0%	100%	0%	100%	100%	0%
Health care and social services	0%	1%	0%	100%	0%	100%	100%	0%
Other public, social, and personal services	20%	2%	0%	0%	0%	100%	0%	0%

Note: Numbers in blue are parameters.

Source: Author's calculations.

In the template provided in Table 19, agricultural goods are subject to a preferential VAT rate of 10%. The total VAT revenue is estimated as 165 billion local currency (LC). To estimate the revenue cost of a 10% VAT rate for agricultural products, the tax rate is replaced with 20%, the standard rate. Table 20 shows the results of the simulations. Repeal of exemptions or preferential tax rates are entered in the parameter template, and the results are shown in the output template. The tax calculator calculates the changes,

Table 20: Result of Repealing the Preferential VAT Rate on Agricultural Products

	Sales (+)	Intermediate Purchases (-)	Purchases of Exempt Goods (+)	Gross Capital Formation (Investments) (-)	Total Supply [1-2]	Taxable Supply [1-2+3-4]	Tax Revenue [1-2+3-4]	VAT Base/ Total Supply	VAT Revenue/ Sales
	1	2	3	4	5	6	7	8	9
Total Supply	4,739,761	2,846,147			1,893,614				
Taxable Supply	3,865,082	2,692,371	153,776	442,761		883,727		46.67%	
Tax Revenue	790,338	527,257	3,407	88,552			177,936		3.75%

VAT = value-added tax.
Source: Author's calculations.

and the results are summarized in the output template. When the agricultural products are taxed at the standard VAT rate of 20%, the expected tax liability is 177.9 billion LC. Therefore, the revenue forgone by providing a lower VAT rate to agricultural goods is 12.9 billion LC. The change in VAT liability of each industry is also available in the table but not shown.

The calculation process of the estimated tax liability can be seen in Table 20 by following the signs in each column heading. First, total supply (sales) and intermediate inputs (purchases) are calculated. Second, purchases of exempt businesses are added because they will not be able to use them as input credits. Third, expenditure on capital goods is deducted because they are not taxed.[36] Then we arrive at the taxable supply ([1]-[2]+[3]-[4]. The VAT tax rate is applied to taxable supply to estimate the tax liability without the preferential VAT rate on agricultural goods.

Discussion of Data Sources

Aggregate National Account Approach

The data for the national account approach are simple and straightforward. All data are obtained from national accounts statistics. However, the data require a significant amount of adjustment before the GDP data can be used as a reasonable proxy for the VAT base.

Subtracting investment and net trade leaves consumption as the gross proxy for the VAT base. However, other data on the amount of zero-rated consumption and purchases of exempt businesses are needed. These can be obtained from household expenditure surveys. In addition, the survey data must be further adjusted by using VAT collections data from tax administration files to find the share of zero-rated and exempt consumption. Therefore, additional data requirement and adjustments for exempt purchases and sales and zero-rated sales can be time-consuming.

[36] For example, it would be convenient to exempt an imported drilling equipment to be used in the production of oil.

Household Survey Approach

The model uses household survey data from the household income and expenditure survey conducted by the national statistics agencies.[37] Household data have be adjusted similarly to the adjustments required for the national accounts approach.

Input–Output Approach Database

The input and output table approach involves building an I–O table, used as the database, and then developing and applying models for revenue simulations. I–O tables are adapted to construct the VAT database. The I–O tables can be augmented by additional data, including trade margins and growth rates by sectors.

Customs and Excises

Generally Accepted Tax Expenditures Under Customs and Excises

In general, World Trade Organization members impose no or very low tariff rates on their imports. The tax burden on imports is usually in the form of VAT, excises, and various customs fees. Members of economic unions implement a so-called common external tariff regime. However, common external tariff rates are usually 0%, 5%, 10%, 15%, and 20%. A few agricultural items may have higher tariff rates.

A key principle of benchmark design is that similar goods should be subject to similar tax rates, regardless of their source. Consequently, the customs duty benchmark should be such that imported goods are subject to the same taxes on consumption as domestically produced goods. That means the benchmark customs tariff rates on goods imported should be zero. Customs tariff revenues in this case would be treated like negative tax expenditures.[38] The tax base of tariff is the cost, insurance, and freight value of imports converted to domestic currency. For some products, weight is considered the tax base in which case the tariff is a specific amount. However, it is common for countries to provide tariff exemptions for various reasons, such as for intermediate products, to provide incentives for domestic and foreign investment.

Exemptions to tariffs are numerous, and tariff exemptions are provided to all the goods that are exempted from VAT. Even though both taxes have different purposes, they are often applied simultaneously. Brenton et al. (2009) estimate that tariff exemptions account for a substantial amount of their tariff revenues. In some countries, tariff exemptions may account for more than 50% of the tariff revenues. This is a substantial amount considering the declining statutory tariff rates worldwide. Furthermore, a substantial portion of the tariff exemptions are granted to importers located in special economic zones (SEZs). Exempting imports from tariffs has implication for VAT. Since tariffs are included in the tax base of VAT on imports, exemptions reduce the taxable base of VAT. This implies significant tax benefits to a small group of taxpayers.

[37] In addition to surveys by the national statistics agencies, the World Bank provides a similar survey called the Living Standards Measurement Survey. The survey is useful in countries where the national statistics agency has limited capacity. The survey, often conducted in cooperation with the national statistics agencies, provides useful data on poverty, heath, and demographic characteristics of households.

[38] For example, Australia treats tariff revenues as negative tax since the benchmark rates are assumed to be zero. See https://treasury.gov.au/sites/default/files/2019-03/2015_TES.pdf.

Excises are generally imposed on alcohol and tobacco products, hydrocarbon products, and a variety of other goods and services. These excises are imposed primarily on the grounds of correcting market failures as with negative externalities, and for distributional and revenue purposes.

Estimation Methodology for Tax Expenditures

Tariff revenues forgone can be estimated using the customs system based on Harmonized System (HS) codes. All imports are registered according to a classification system used worldwide. Imports according to the HS codes are registered up to the 12-digit level. Customs administration records for each commodity imported, the cost, insurance, and freight value of the imported good; its quantity; import tariff paid; exempted amount if exempted according to the Customs Code; excise tax if applicable; VAT paid; customs service charge; and exemption for VAT and excises. Therefore, summing up all the exempted tariff revenues would provide the amount of tariff revenues forgone for any particular year.

However, a simple tabulation of all the statutory tariff exemptions may not account for all the revenues forgone. Since tariff exemptions change the price of imported goods, they may result in the change of quantity of goods imported and domestically produced. It may result in a substitution effect for some products being imported rather than domestically produced. Such effects can be better captured using a trade model that considers behavioral effects.

Hypothetical Calculation for Tax Expenditures

The calculation of revenue cost of tax expenditures at the customs is straightforward. Customs administrations maintain detailed databases on the goods imported, including their value and weight, tariff payments, VAT and excise payments, and exemptions or reduced tariffs. However, these data are very detailed and have to be summarized.

Given the data availability, revenue cost of tax expenditures can be calculated by summing up the recorded exemptions by each type of tax across all imported goods. Table 21 demonstrates a sample of data available at customs compiled by the Automated System for Customs Data (ASYCUDA) system in addition to other data.[39] The revenue losses due to exemptions are equal to the value of duties and taxes forgone reported in Table 21. They can be summed up to obtain the total revenues forgone at the customs. A simplified version of tax expenditures is presented in Table 22. Revenue forgone is estimated as the difference between calculated tax liability and what is actually paid after the tax benefits.[40]

Discussion of Data Sources

Customs administrations collect data on imported goods according to internationally accepted product codes. These codes can be up to 12 digits and provide highly detailed data. For each imported product, its weight, value, and tariff rate from the tariff book are all recorded. In addition, VAT liability and excise liability are also recorded, if they are due. Some duties or excises can be specific rates on the quantity imported. Furthermore, all the exemptions by type of tax are also recorded. Customs administrations have the capacity to produce these databases within a day and make it available for tax expenditure analysis.

[39] ASYCUDA was developed to standardize customs data according to the HS. The system includes a lot of information on imported goods in addition to value of import, duties, fees, and taxes.

[40] See Laporte et al. (2018).

Table 21: Calculated Exemptions of Hypothetical Customs Exemptions

	Two-Digit Harmonization Code (HS)	Imports (value)	Weight (kg)	Import Duty	Excises	VAT	Exempted Import Duty	Exempted Excise	Exempted VAT
1	Aircraft, spacecraft, and parts	22,693,961	54,237	354,942	-	599,939	4,183,850	-	2,920,365
2	Albuminoidal subs, starches, enzymes	40,307,604	7,768,916	4,900,697	-	5,908,324	3,146,803	-	938,882
3	Aluminum and articles	373,220,381	34,442,080	22,211,545	5	40,550,096	31,873,332	-	19,217,038
4	Animal or vegetable Fats, oils and waxes	552,568,084	203,570,851	56,551,805	-	88,312,602	22,780,602	-	3,178,216
5	Arms and ammunition, parts and accessories	638,633,617	1,946,773	2,918,876	-	2,626,989	124,807,240	-	111,477,999
6	Apparel and clothing accessories – knitted	63,508,696	4,881,840	8,277,407	-	7,446,882	4,420,608	-	3,568,249
7	Apparel and clothing access. – not knitted	62,421,317	7,454,732	10,154,496	-	9,145,376	2,322,223	-	1,777,552
8	Articles of iron or steel	2,063,659,245	236,662,243	71,316,642	-	83,342,551	182,369,697	-	236,378,719
9	Articles of leather, handbags, etc.	88,263,140	23,148,561	17,047,913	-	15,377,898	597,556	-	449,287
10	Articles of stone, plaster, cement, asbest	92,420,921	37,917,322	6,808,944	-	9,303,866	4,325,892	-	5,674,715
11	Base metals nesoi, cermets, articles, etc.	1,996,948	92,264	84,907	-	73,445	312,959	-	242,046
12	Beverages, spirits and vinegar	317,249,694	113,158,478	53,987,001	51,370,831	63,085,494	9,195,891	341,794	1,569,325
13	Carpets and other textile floor coverings	9,470,922	1,509,295	1,483,347	-	1,576,349	410,837	-	120,751
14	Ceramic products	500,041,915	403,040,983	44,861,819	-	71,978,188	6,832,075	-	10,390,214
15	Cereals	1,767,926,630	1,181,371,760	244,649,872	298	244,106,262	53,886,708	-	57,548,122
16	Clocks, watches, and parts	4,811,467	588,887	815,034	-	733,762	147,259	-	113,809
17	Cocoa and cocoa preparations	41,080,267	7,882,011	3,857,140	-	4,200,227	4,359,692	-	2,700,828
18	Coffee, tea, mate, and spices	28,155,749	19,686,823	4,282,273	-	4,625,489	1,336,092	-	263,790
19	Copper and articles	95,764,854	4,484,059	3,550,530	-	6,853,593	6,989,300	-	8,167,382
	.	.	.	.	.	.	.	.	.
	.	.	.	.	.	.	.	.	.
	.	.	.	.	.	.	.	.	.
	Grand Total	40,258,808,935	11,954,656,927	2,266,478,903	106,784,653	3,332,943,339	1,609,895,196	342,191	1,721,055,357

HS = Harmonized System, kg = kilogram, VAT = value-added tax.

Source: Author's calculations.

Table 22: Effect of Tax Expenditures on Customs Exemptions

Harmonization Code (HS)	Imports (value)	Weight (kg)	Other Fees and Dues	Import Duty Rate (%)	Import Duty	Exempted Import Duty	Import Duty Paid	Excises	Exempted Excise	VAT Rate (%)	VAT	Exempted VAT	VAT Paid
	(1)	(2)	(3)	(4)	[(5)=(1)*(4)]	(6)	(7)=[(5)-(6)]	(8)	(9)	(10)	[(11)=(10)*{(1)+(5)+(8)}]	(12)	[(13)=(11)-(12)]
Apparel and Clothing	63,508,696	4,881,840	3,260,849	15	9,526,304	4,420,608	5,105,696	0	0	15	10,292,159	3,568,249	6,723,910
Ceramic Products	500,041,915	403,040,983	12,344,259	10	50,004,192	6,832,075	43,172,117	0	0	15	81,482,105	10,390,214	71,091,891
Cereals	1,767,926,630	1,181,371,760	30,384,403	15	265,188,995	53,886,708	211,302,286	298	0	15	296,884,382	57,548,122	239,336,260
Total	2,331,477,241	1,589,294,583	45,989,511	15	349,721,586	65,139,391	284,582,195	298	0	15	392,408,960	71,506,586	317,152,060

HS = Harmonized System, kg = kilogram, VAT = value-added tax.

Source: Author's calculations.

Table 23: Template for Customs Data Requirements for Tax Expenditure Calculations

Taxes and fees, and exemptions, at customs, by product

Data for 2022 (or most recent tax year for which data are available)

Data are grouped by product type (each row corresponds to a different product)

LC Local Currency

				Taxes and Fees Payable – Statutory Tax Rates				Total Taxes and Fees Payable – Amounts in LC				Total Exemptions – Amounts in LC			
HS 4 Product Code	Product Name	Total Import CIF Value (LC)	Total Weight (tons)	Vat Rate (% CIF value)	Excise Rate (% CIF value)	Duty (tariff) Rate (% CIF value)	Duty (tariff) Rate (per ton)	Vat	Excises	Duties	Fees/ Charges	Vat	Excises	Duties	Fees/ Charges
1517															
1518															
1519															
1520															
1521															
.	.	.	.	.	.	.	.	.	.	.	.	.	.	.	.

CIF = cost, insurance, and freight; HS = Harmonized System, LC = local currency; VAT = value-added tax.

Source: Author's calculations.

It should be noted that some exemptions or reduced rates at customs may be the result of a free trade agreement or a double taxation agreement. In these cases, the exemptions or preferential rates should be considered part of the benchmark system. Also, any preferential rate or exemption provided to imports from trading partners within a common external tariff is not considered a tax expenditure. It is international practice to exempt imports by diplomatic missions and international organizations as final users. Their imports are exempt from indirect taxes including customs duties, VAT, and excises; therefore, they are not considered tax expenditures.

Countries or international agencies often request exemptions from indirect taxes (e.g., customs duties, VAT) or income taxes (e.g., personal income tax [PIT] and corporate income tax [CIT]) for development assistance-financed goods and services they provide to developing countries. Most European Union countries, the United States, and Canada ask for exemptions. It has not always been clear which goods and services financed by development agencies are exempt from taxation. What is exempted is often negotiated. This may impact the revenue mobilization effort of developing countries. In some cases, the exemptions are extended to private businesses undertaking projects on behalf of international agencies. This can result in significant revenue losses. The United Nations has issued guidelines on tax treatment of international assistance.[41] Table 23 displays key items needed from customs to estimate the tax expenditures by HS code.

[41] See United Nations (2021).

6 TAX EXPENDITURE PRACTICE IN SELECTED ASIAN COUNTRIES

Governments use tax expenditures with the aim of achieving certain objectives, such as promoting growth and social welfare, attracting investment. Among Asian Development Bank members, only nine report tax expenditures.[42] The revenue cost of tax expenditure in Asian countries is about 3.5% of GDP on average. Most of the forgone revenues come from tax expenditures provided under VAT, followed by taxes on profits. PIT is low because few have effective taxes on income.[43] Table 24 shows the revenues forgone as share of GDP in Asian countries.

Table 24: Tax Expenditures by Country

		% of GDP (2020)
		2020
1	Pakistan	2.8
2	India	0.4
3	Indonesia	1.5
4	Philippines	2.6
5	Mongolia	1.6
6	Republic of Korea	2.8
7	New Zealand	1.4
8	Russian Federation	14.8
9	Australia	7.92
	Average	3.5

GDP = gross domestic product.
Source: Global Tax Expenditure Database.

Australia, India, New Zealand, and Pakistan provide detailed tax expenditure reports. These reports are useful in guiding tax policy. While estimation methodologies may differ, all tax expenditure reports provide useful indicators such as revenues forgone as share of GDP and total tax revenues. In all cases, estimates are limited by the amount and accuracy of the available data. Some countries such as Australia and New Zealand have been highly experienced in providing tax expenditure reports since the early 1980s.

Australia has over 200 concessions that it identifies as tax expenditures, totaling about 4% of GDP. Tax expenditures are estimated using various types of models. Aggregate models are used in estimating revenue forgone for tax expenditures that can be captured from national accounts used in the calculation of excise tax expenditures on fuels. To estimate cost of concessions for taxpayer groups, distributional models are used. Data sources for distributional modeling include survey data as well as taxpayer data from tax administration files. These tax concessions are provided to demographic groups as well as individuals in

42 See Redonda, von Haldenwang, and Aliu (2022).

43 See Gupta and Jalles (2022).

low-income classes. In addition, microsimulation models based on taxpayer data are used to estimate the cost of tax expenditures for individuals as well as corporations.

The benchmark in Australian tax expenditure estimation is based on the Haig–Simons definition of income. Benchmarks are defined for PIT, retirement benefits, fringe benefits tax, business tax, and excise tax. No tax expenditure report is provided for goods and services tax, a kind of VAT, because it is considered a tax for states and territories.[44]

New Zealand does not have a long list of tax expenditures. Tax expenditures account for about 1.4% of GDP. Most of the tax concessions support social activities and individuals, mostly in the form of tax credits. Tax expenditures for businesses support livestock, environment, and scientific research. New Zealand does not define a benchmark based on some norms. The main objective is to provide tax relief to targeted groups.

Tax expenditures in Pakistan are numerous. Income tax expenditures can be grouped under allowances, tax credits, exemptions, reduced rates, and reduced liabilities. Sales tax expenditures are in the form of exemptions and reduced tax rates. Similarly, exemptions at customs are also in the form of exemptions.[45]

Data for income tax estimations are obtained from income tax returns or other agencies including social security administration and the private sector. Revenues forgone are calculated by aggregating the data from the tax returns submitted by taxpayers or provided by third parties such as the statistics agencies. The revenues forgone are estimated first by applying the current law parameters to the database obtained from these data sources. Then, the revenues are calculated without the tax expenditure items individually. The revenues forgone are estimated as the difference between the benchmark and the recalculated tax liability without the tax expenditure.

To estimate the sales tax expenditures, the data on sales tax returns were retrieved from tax administration at an aggregate level. First, the tax base was established, and the revenues forgone are estimated by applying the statutory rate of 17%. The estimates ignore the behavioral response to repeal of a tax expenditure, which is a common practice.

The Philippines has made several attempts to publish a tax expenditure report but has not produced it yet. The country's tax code provides numerous tax expenditures so developing capacity to produce a tax expenditure report would be useful in providing guidance to tax policy. However, the Department of Finance and the Bureau of Internal Revenue provide estimates of tax expenditures on investment incentives.

[44] See Commonwealth of Australia, Ministry of Treasury and Economic Development (2015).

[45] See Pakistan Federal Board of Revenue (2021).

7 STATISTICAL ISSUES FOR MODELING OF TAX EXPENDITURES

In microsimulation modeling, for computational and accuracy reasons, creating a representative sample of taxpayers rather than implementing a simulation on the total population of taxpayers is much more efficient. Once the simulations are implemented on the sampled data files, the results are blown up to population totals by applying the weight to each representative taxpayer in the sample. Therefore, the taxpayer population has to be sampled. However, some criteria are required to guarantee the accuracy of the simulation results. In the case of PIT, tax returns can be randomly selected according to the size of income and demographic characteristics, such as married and unmarried. In CIT, the firms in the sample can be selected according to the type of industry they operate in, or the size of assets and/or revenues.

These samples have to be selected randomly, and the sample should have an acceptable level of accuracy. Sampling enables analysts to make inferences about the population they are studying. The observations selected in the sample represent the likelihood of the occurrence of that element in the population. There are different types of sampling based on the objectives of sample design and the costs associated with selecting the sample. The three most common methods of sampling are described in this section. Additional sampling methods are explained in Appendix 2.

Simple Random Sampling

Simple random sampling is a probability sampling method where the sample observations are randomly drawn from a population. The observations in a population are randomly selected to make inferences about the characteristics of the population. In a randomly selected sample, each observation has the same probability of being selected in the sample. The likelihood of being included in the sample equals 1 divided by the total number of observations in the population. If the sample size is "n," the likelihood of an observation to be included in the sample is $p=n/N$, where "N" is the number of all observations in the population.

Suppose in a study of households, 1,000 households are randomly selected from a population of 100,000 households. The probability p of selection for any given individual will be $p = 1{,}000/100{,}000 = .001$ (or 0.1%). That means 1 out of every 1,000 households will be selected randomly.

This method requires that the observations in the population are known. In sampling taxpayers, sampling can be easily done since the total number of taxpayers and their attributes are known. Once the total number of observations in the population is known, random numbers can be assigned to each observation. Using a random number generator, the observations can be selected until the sample size is reached. While it is simple, simple random sampling may not be sufficient to select a sample of representative taxpayers because it ignores some of the characteristics of the taxpayer population.

Systematic Sampling

Systematic sampling is like simple random sampling where the sample is selected in a predetermined order from a randomly distributed population. Once the entire population is known, it should be distributed randomly. Then, a starting point is selected randomly. After the determination of the first observation to be selected, the remaining observations are selected systematically by selecting every i^{th} observation.

Assume that every 20th observation is to be selected from a population of 1,000. If the starting point 7 is selected randomly, the observations 27th, 47th, 67th, 87th, etc. are selected. The sampling interval is determined by dividing the number of observations in the population by the number of observations to be included in the sample. In the case of selecting a sample of 50 observations out of a population of 1,000, the sampling interval would be 1,000/50=20 (number of observations in the population/size of the sample).

Stratified Sampling

Stratified sampling is used to assure the representation of each subgroup in the sample. Before sampling, a sample design divides the population into strata according to the characteristics of the observations. In the case of sampling taxpayers, they can be stratified according to the size of income, type of income (labor income and non-labor income), and type of household (married or single). It should be noted that as the number of strata increases, the number of observations to be included in the sample also increases to achieve a desirable level of precision. Appendix 2 describes the steps in determining the sample size and the size of each stratum for a given level of precision (e.g., an error level of 3%).

Once the strata are determined and the overall precision level of the sample is known, the observations from each stratum are randomly selected for the sample. This sampling procedure would minimize the standard deviation of the observations in each stratum and increase the precision of estimates. The number of observations selected for the sample can be proportional to the relative size of each group within the population.

Assume a sample of 100 taxpayers are to be selected from a population of 1,000 taxpayers. The taxpayers are divided into three groups by size of income: low, middle, and high income. The share of taxpayers in each income bracket are 0.2, 0.7, and 0.1. The size of each stratum in the sample will be as follows:

First stratum = 1,000 * 0.2 = 20
Second stratum = 1,000 * 0.7 = 70
Third stratum = 1,000 * 0.1 = 10

This method is known as proportional sampling. However, some observations may be underrepresented in this case, resulting in inaccurate estimation of these groups. In this case, the sampling rates have to be increased. As shown in Appendix 2, the size of each stratum depends on the variance (standard deviation) of the observations within that stratum. The higher the variance of the selection criteria, the larger is the number of observations to be included in the sample. For example, when sampling taxpayers according to their income, proportional sampling may underrepresent high-income taxpayers because there are fewer of them compared with other income groups. In this case, the number of sampled observations for this group of taxpayers would have to be increased according to the variance of the taxpayers in the high-income brackets.

The best practice for sampling taxpayers for microsimulation modeling is stratified sampling, where taxpayers are divided into strata that reflect their economic and demographic characteristics. The most important criterion is the level of total income for PIT sample selection. For CIT, the population of firms has to be divided into industry, asset size, and revenues. Industry classification may not be essential, unless the microsimulation requires that certain industries are properly represented in the sample.

Sample size should be decided based on a margin of error. If a sampling error of 3% is acceptable, then the size (n) of the sample for simple random sampling becomes

$$n = \frac{N}{(1+Ne^2)}$$

where N is the size of population and e is the margin of error. For example, for e=3% and

$$N = 100{,}000{,}000 \;\; => \;\; n = 1{,}111$$

Once the sample is selected, the tax information on the sampled taxpayers must be verified for accuracy. Each stratum should closely represent the stratum it comes from in the population. For example, does the sample, when weighted, produce an accurate estimate of the total tax liability? Does the sample estimate the tax liability of the population accurately in each stratum when weighted?

The sample selection step for stratified sampling is explained in Appendix 2. The distribution of the sample should represent the distribution of the population. Usually, it is difficult to represent tail ends. Therefore, the upper end of the distribution should be sampled at rates close to 100%. If there exist inaccuracies at the lower end of the distribution of taxpayers, then resampling the stratum would reduce the sampling errors.

Figure 2: Relationship between Sample Size and Sampling Error

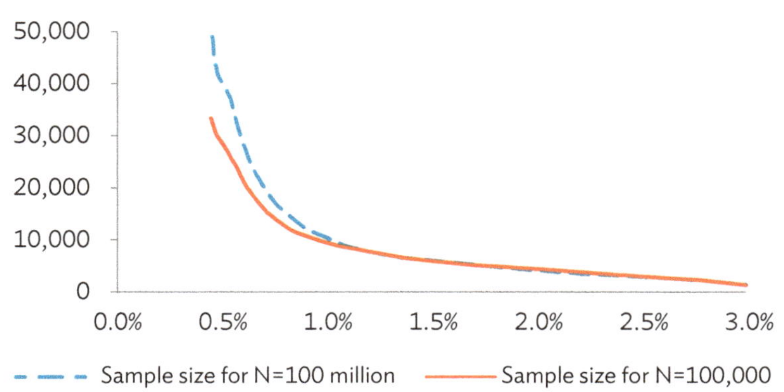

Source: Author's calculations.

APPENDIX 1

MEASUREMENT OF MARGINAL EFFECTIVE TAX RATES

Marginal effective tax rates (METRs) may be derived from a simple model of investment, where managers of a representative firm make investment decisions geared at maximizing profit net of corporate-level tax. For a given set of tax rates, interest (discount) rates and prices, the representative firm is assumed to raise equity capital sufficient to invest at the outset of the current period in the optimal (profit-maximizing) capital stock. Managers are also assumed to have static expectations regarding tax rates—they assume that tax rates are unchanged, until such time when a new tax policy (e.g., introduction of a tax incentive) is introduced. At such time, the firm adjusts to a new optimal capital stock level.

The model assumes a single stock of physical capital which depreciates at a declining-balance rate (δ), which may differ from the rate of depreciation allowed for tax purposes (α). In each year, replacement investment ($I_t=\delta^*K_t$) maintains the capital stock at its optimal level.

Under these assumptions, the net present value of the after-tax cash flow from investment may be measured as follows:

$$NPV = -Q_0 I_0 (1-uA) + \sum_{t=1}^{\infty} \frac{P_t F(K_t)(1-u) - (1-uA)Q_t I_t}{((1+r)(1+\pi))^t} \qquad (1)$$

where (r) is the minimum (normal) real rate of return net of corporate tax required by shareholders, (π) is the rate of inflation, (u) is the statutory profit tax rate, and (A) measures the present value of tax relief from depreciation allowances plus investment tax credit (if any) per currency unit of investment. With declining-balance tax depreciation, A is measured by

$$A = \sum_{s=1}^{\infty} \frac{\alpha(1-\alpha)^{s-1}}{[(1+r)(1+\pi)]^{s-1}} = \alpha \frac{(1+r)(1+\pi)}{r(1+\pi)+\pi+\alpha} \qquad (2)$$

where (α) is the tax depreciation rate. The ratio in (2) is the net present value of tax depreciation allowances per currency unit of investment (uZ).

Under the assumption of immediate adjustment to the profit-maximizing capital stock, and replacement investment each year to maintain that stock, the net present value expression (1) reduces to the following (with market prices normalized, such that $P_0=Q_0=1$):

$$NPV = \frac{(1-u)F(K)-(r+\delta)(1-uA)K}{r} = \frac{(1-u)\left[\frac{F(K)}{K}-\delta\right]-(r+\delta)(1-uA)}{r}K \qquad (3)$$

A real gross rate of return net of depreciation can be written after differentiating net present value with respect to K as

$$RG = F_K - \delta = (r+\delta)\frac{1-uA}{1-u} - \delta \qquad (4)$$

Tax distortions to the level of investment are assessed using the following marginal effective tax rate:

$$METR = \frac{RG - r}{RG} = \frac{(F_K - \delta) - r}{RG} = \frac{F_K - (r + \delta)}{RG} = \frac{u(1 - A)(r + \delta)}{r(1 - uA) + u\delta(1 - A)} \qquad (5)$$

While the marginal product of capital F_K is in general unobservable, it can be inferred from the profit maximizing condition, equating F_K with the user cost of capital.

Some stylized results can be shown, such as when there is no tax, $RG=r$. When $A = 1$ then tax is neutral, again $RG=r$. In general, where $A>1$, $RG>r$ and METR is positive implying a burden on investment.

APPENDIX 2

SAMPLE SIZE SELECTION METHODOLOGY FOR STRATIFIED SAMPLING

Determination of Sample Size:

1. Calculate mean $w_h = \frac{n_h}{N}$ for each stratum, μ_h, where h is the index of the number of strata and N_h is the number of observations in stratum h, and L is the total number of strata. Then, calculate overall mean.

$$\mu_{ST} = \sum_{h=1}^{L} \frac{N_h}{N} \mu_h$$

2. Calculate stratified standard error of the stratified sample where s_h^2 is the strata variance and $w_h = \frac{n_h}{N}$ is the weight or share of each stratum.

$$SE_{ST}^2 = \sum_{h=1}^{L} (w_h^{\ 2} \frac{s_h^2}{N_h})$$

3. Confidence interval

$$\mu_{ST} \pm t_{1-\alpha} * SE_{ST}$$

where $t_{1-\alpha}$ = 2.05 for 95% confidence interval (for 99% t = 2.58).

4. Precision (Coefficient of Variation):

$$CV_{ST} = \frac{t_{1-\alpha} * SE_{ST}}{\mu_{ST}}$$

5. Sample size: Select an acceptable error level, E.

$$n = \frac{t^2}{E^2} \left(\sum_{h=1}^{L} w_h s_h) \right)^2$$

For example, set E = 10% (or E = 1%). Convert to absolute terms, i.e., $E = 10\% * \mu_{ST}$.

6. Allocate the sample size to strata.

$$n_h = n \frac{w_h s_h}{\sum_{h=1}^{L} (w_h s_h)}$$

Additional Sampling Methods:[1]

Cluster Sampling

In cluster sampling, the population is divided into groups that have characteristics similar to the population. The clusters are separated from each other by one or more attributes. These attributes can be geographic groupings, i.e., groups of households located in different regions or firms classified by type of industry. The clusters can be large in number. Then the clusters are randomly selected to form the sample that represents the population.

Cluster sampling is more cost-effective but less accurate compared to stratified sampling. The main difference between cluster sampling and stratified sampling is that in cluster sampling, the cluster is the sampling unit selected, whereas in stratified sampling, observations to be included in the sample are chosen within each stratum. Cluster samples are formed first by dividing the population of observations into clusters (groups), then some observations from each cluster are randomly selected to form the sample.

Multistage Sampling

In multistage sampling, observations to be included in the final sample are selected in stages. The population is divided into different groupings that form the first sampling stage. The groupings can be like clusters based on region, or another type of association such as type of business formation. The primary samples are further sampled into smaller groupings forming the following stages of sampling. At each stage, the sample groups become smaller.

This sampling technique is useful when the size of the population is unknown. Multistage sampling is commonly used in household surveys where households are first grouped into regions (e.g., urban and nonurban areas) at the first stage. Then, the regions are further grouped into smaller sampling units, the districts. Further, divisions into neighborhoods and blocks constitute later stages of sampling. Then, households are randomly selected from each subsample. Adding more stages improves the sampling accuracy of the final sample selected.

1 For further reading on sampling, see Cochran (1977).

REFERENCES

Abbas, S., A. Klemm, S. Bedi, and J. Park. 2012. A Partial Race to the Bottom: Corporate Tax Developments in Emerging and Developing Economies. *IMF Working Paper*. WP/12/2.

Beer, S., D. Benedek, B. Erard, and J. Loeprick. 2022. Tax Expenditure Reporting and Its Use in Fiscal Management: A Guide for Developing Economies. *How to Notes.* No. 22/05. Fiscal Affairs Department, International Monetary Fund.

Brenton, P., C. Saborowski, C. Staritz, and E. von Uexkull. 2009. Assessing the Adjustment Implications of Trade Policy Changes Using TRIST. *World Bank Policy Research Working Paper.* 5045.

Brown, C. 2004. Tax Expenditures in Australia. In Brixi, H. P., C. M. A. Valenduc, and Z. L. Swift, eds. *Tax Expenditures – Shedding Light on Government Spending Through the Tax System: Lessons from Developed and Transition Economies*. Washington, DC: World Bank.

Cochran, G. W. 1977. *Sampling Techniques*. John Wiley and Sons.

Commonwealth of Australia, Ministry of Treasury and Economic Development. 2015. Tax Expenditure Statement, 2015. https://treasury.gov.au/sites/default/files/2019-03/2015_TES.pdf.

Craig, J. and W. Allan. 2001. Fiscal Transparency, Tax Expenditures, and Budget Processes: An International Perspective. *NTA Papers and Proceedings*.

Ebrill, L., M. Keen, J.P. Bodin, and V. Summers. 2001. *The Modern VAT*. Washington, DC: International Monetary Fund.

Global Tax Expenditure Database. https://gted.taxexpenditures.org/.

Gupta, S. and J. T. Jalles. 2022. Priorities for Strengthening Key Revenue Sources in Asia. https://www.cgdev.org/sites/default/files/priorities-strengthening-key-revenue-sources-asia.pdf.

Heady, C. and M. Mansour. 2019. Tax Expenditure Reporting and Its Use in Fiscal Management: A Guide for Developing Economies. *How to Notes.* No. 19/01. Fiscal Affairs Department, International Monetary Fund.

Hutton, E. 2010. A Basic Framework for Evaluating Value Added Tax Expenditures. *Inter-American Development Bank Discussion Paper*. IDB-DP-138. https://publications.iadb.org/ publications/english/document/A-Basic-Framework-for-Evaluating-Value-Added-Tax-Expenditures.pdf.

Klemm, A. 2006. Allowances for Corporate Equity in Practice. *IMF Working Paper*. WP/06/259.

Laporte, B., E. Caldeira, C. de Quatrebarbes, and Y. Bouterige. 2018. *Tax Expenditure Assessment: From Principles to Practice: Methodological Guide*. Fondation pour les Études et Recherches sur le Développement International (Ferdi).

Le, T. M. 2007. Estimating the VAT Base: Method and Application. 9 April. *Tax Notes International*. Washington, DC. p. 203.

Organisation for Economic Co-operation and Development (OECD). 1996. *Tax Expenditures. Recent Experiences*. Paris.

———. 2004. *Best Practice Guidelines – Off Budget and Tax Expenditures*. Paris.

———. 2010. Choosing a Broad Base- Low-Rate Approach to Taxation. *Tax Policy Studies*. No. 19. Paris.

Pakistan Federal Board of Revenue. 2021. Tax Expenditure Report.

Phillips, D., Y. Tyskerud, and R. Warwick. 2021. *An Introduction to Tax Policy Costing: A Manual and Worked Examples*. The Institute for Fiscal Studies.

Redonda, A., C. von Haldenwang, and F. Aliu. 2022. Global Tax Expenditures Database [data set], Version 1.1.3. https://doi.org/10.5281/zenodo.6334212.

United Nations. 2021. *Guidelines on the Tax Treatment of Government-to-Government Aid Projects*. New York.

www.ingramcontent.com/pod-product-compliance
Lightning Source LLC
Chambersburg PA
CBHW041758220926
51847CB00014B/247
* 9 7 8 9 2 9 2 7 0 5 5 1 0 *